Being "Pickity"

By Wendy Walter

Wendy Walter

"Once in a while, right in the middle of an ordinary life, love gives us a fairytale."

To Judith and David,
who distilled "Being Pickity"
into a place, and were brave enough
to share it with us.

I honor YOU, stream of consciousness
through which our ancestors came and went;
from which present relatives perceive, and into
which future family generations will create.
Thank you for this unique family experience.

Table of Contents
Life Cycle of the Garden

Prologue

Pickity Place is a New Hampshire landmark created by my parents, Judith and David Walter, in 1976. Ten acres of land, a foundation of gardens, an old carriage shed, a small greenhouse, and a red colonial home were ideal for the self-sufficient family. The magic of the property was immediately recognized by my parents and was a natural setting for an idyllic childhood. It provided trees, fresh air, herbs, delicious food, a slew of pets, and a lot of play time.

We were raised in the woods of Mason, New Hampshire, immersed in my parent's vision of simplicity and beauty. Nutrient-dense, balanced soil is where plants will thrive. A childhood rich with creativity and imagination was not without its arguments, sibling rivalry, teen angst, and parental discontent. Nonetheless, I was incredibly lucky to have been planted in that 'soil' of place and time, to soak up that particular reality. Only my siblings can relate to a truly "Pickity" upbringing, as the business grew out of our family's beliefs and dreams.

Mentioning the name "Pickity Place" almost always evokes 'oohs' and 'ahhs'. When I reveal I grew up there, people feel compelled to share their Pickity stories; when they go, how often, and how much it means to them. Sharing stories has a way of creating community and connection. It's my hope that, as I honor my parents story, you remember the love, strength, and power of your story and your own sense of "Being Pickity".

The Seed and The Soil

If you build up the soil with organic material, the plants will do just fine.

John Harrison

Dusk. A lone car snakes up a long dirt driveway to a red 1700's colonial house nestled beneath a giant ash tree. The couple decide this is the place before they even get out of the car. It simply feels like home. With just enough light remaining, they see gardens to resurrect, 10 acres for kids and animals to roam, a carriage barn to convert, and an old, somewhat rickety house. The best surprise - it was the real-life fairy tale setting as Grandmother's house in a Golden Book version of *Little Red Riding Hood*. Judith Walter was excited, but skeptical - would people travel this far to a shop in the woods?

Several real estate agents had given up helping the Walters find the perfect location. For three frustrating years, the couple searched all over southern New Hampshire, from Keene to Hollis, for a place to start a craft shop and farm. On the verge of letting go of their dream, David and Judith reluctantly agreed to view one more property. And on that fateful evening in 1974, Judith knew this was it. At long last, their quest had come to an end. They had found the location to create a "Pickity Place".

The town of Mason, where they found themselves, was populated by about 610 people. It offered a quiet, remote destination. Established in 1621, the town of Mason was named after Captain John Mason who took on land ownership and settlement endeavors, single-handedly, in New Hampshire. "No individual can be found who exhibited more courage or perseverance in the cause, or more confidence in its ultimate success, or who expended his means with a more liberal hand in promoting the settlement of the country."[1]

New Hampshire is also named after Captain Mason's birth place, the county of Hampshire, in England, where he was the Governor of Portsmouth. Captain Mason set a precedent for New Englanders ~ entrepreneurial, courageous, and persistent; qualities Judith and David embody.

More than a century after Captain Mason's influence in New Hampshire, Ebenezer Blood arrived in Mason in 1759 and built the colonial home now known as Pickity Place. His daughter Naomi and her husband Oliver Nutting were the first to settle in the house on what would be named Nutting Hill. Their son, Eli Nutting, later sold the property to his nephew, Marshall H. Nutting. Another family member possibly owned it after Marshall, but it was ultimately sold to Llmari Muhover from Finland. Dr. James and Marion B. Hitchcock bought the property from Muhover and renovated the interior. They also allowed the fields to revert to woods and established affluent gardens around the house. The Hitchcocks sold their home in 1963 to the Letart Family, who, in 1974, sold it to the Walter's.

The Walter's saw a lot of potential despite the neglect of time. Judith knew how to tend a garden and was excited to bring these back, but was unaware that the soil itself set a paradigm for productivity and a full harvest. New Hampshire's soil, called Marlow, is a well-drained, very firm substratum of basal till deposited about 15,000 years ago by glaciers. It provides some of the most fertile, rich soils for farmers and foresters in the harsh granite landscape.

Entering the world of Pickity Place circa 1975

As the stage was being set in Mason, the Walters were growing up. Judith's story begins in New Hampshire. Certain people, like plants, are meant for a northeastern climate. Judith's parents and grandparents, born and raised in the Granite State, lived what we'd call a 'back to basics' lifestyle. They built their own houses, hunted for their food, canned the vegetables they grew, and crafted the tools they needed to survive. Judith's grandfather, Elverton Berry (1883-1952) for example, passed down his quiet nature, devotion, and deeply rooted connection to the land to his sons Robert, Jim, and Roger Berry. His first wife, Jessie Morgan, (who later became Jessie Wentworth), was known as 'Bela' to Judith and her sisters. A very kind grandmother, she influenced Judith's love of gardening and reading. Tall pink Cosmos and the smell of Petunias are her legacy, while the books *Mary Poppins* and *The Secret Garden* are cherished by Judith as memorable gifts.

Judith's father, Robert Morgan Berry (born in Farmington, New Hampshire), learned his trade from his father, Elverton Berry, as a deputy officer for the New Hampshire Fish and Game Department. Elverton was renowned for his knowledge and is remembered in *Smoke from a Thousand Campfires*, by Paul T. Doherty:

> *"Mr. Berry's enforcement background went back to the days of the fish and game detectives, a time he called the horse and buggy days. He would speak about the times, when ordered to the North Country in winter on an investigation; you took the train as far as Berlin, put on snowshoes and walked the rest of the way up and over Dixville Notch. Known as 'Bert' he was the finest naturalist that has ever worked for New Hampshire's Fish and Game department. His knowledge was mind boggling, yet you would never know it for he had little to say. One soon learned not to push, but to drift into it easy like and get a topic started, then this remarkable man would hold you spellbound.*
>
> *As a powerful backpacker, after the first World War, he carried fingerling trout into many sections of the Passaconaway Valley. For years, fishermen would enjoy the success of his efforts. He would also practice game management long before it was a household word, thinking nothing of roaming a vast tract of land on foot in summer, on snowshoes in winter. He would say that those early days of watching and learning would help develop the tremendous amount of knowledge that filled his head."* (Doherty, p.89).

Following in his father's footsteps, Robert drove a fish truck to stock local ponds and lakes and was called on to look for deer-jackers and other animal poachers. He hunted partridge and enjoyed keeping quite a large vegetable garden. He was also known as a talented artist, painting life-like fish for the NH Fish and Game Department and building a workshop for handcrafting canoes and outhouses.

Judith

Flower patterns of green
or brown lace hinged to edges
hangs from her shoulders down.
She doesn't like the waist ties.

More petals dried, and leaves
hung from old, rustic beams
or on used door screens fill
my world with earthy scents.

Life trails new behind her,
A motley garden of hues:
Hyacinths and Poppies,
Lamb's Ears and Sage.

Bent over, hands immersed
In our farm's dirt
She digs and plants
What I know as home.

Wendy Walter
1988 at Skidmore College

(left) Judy 5 years old, photo taken at the dime store in Meredith, NH; Judy age 16, a junior at the Quimby School in Center Sandwich, NH; (above) Robert Berry Artwork Pickerel, Trout, Woodcock, Ruffed Grouse, White Tailed Deer

Judith's mother, Marion Josephine Nickles (1911-1997) and her predecessors also exemplified tenacious, quiet, hard- working Granite Staters. Born and raised in Candia, Marion attended the Keene Teachers College (known as 'The Keene Normal School' back then). She taught in Colebrook, where she met and married Robert (1932). They moved to Center Sandwich, where Marion taught all eight grades in a one-room school house. "In the fall of 1949, the North Sandwich School opened with twenty students in grades one through six, with Marion Berry as teacher".[2] She later taught third and fourth grade for many years at the Sandwich Central School

Marion kept her feelings to herself, did her duty as a parent, and wasn't one for affection. She tended her terrace garden of Petunias and annuals and loved to clip recipes out of the newspaper to try them. She was an expert seamstress, making her girls' coats and quilts. She canned the vegetables harvested from their garden and kept the household running efficiently. Both she and Robert were prudent, practical, and tenacious Yankees. They kept to themselves and unwittingly enriched the soil for Judith's growth.

Judith was born in Plymouth, New Hampshire on January 5th,1943. She grew up in Sandwich with her two sisters, Fran and Joan. The parsonage in the center of town was home until she was seven, when her father built a house on Dale Road. There, Judy roamed the woods at will, weaving herself into nature; the trees her second family. Pine and smooth birchbark siblings protected her as she discovered the plants and animals her parents and grandparents knew so well.

Northern New Hampshire was sparsely populated in those days, offering clean air and water, abundant trees, plant life, and quiet, pure moments of connection to nature. Children played outside and, more often than not, made their own toys. Judith's youth was imprinted with practicality, innovation, and self-reliance.

Creativity came naturally to Judith; gardening and cooking her favorites, and she imagined herself finding a way to make a living at what she loved. But her father, adamant Judith should make a living doing something practical, determined she would become a teacher. She was sent to Plymouth Teacher College for a B.ED, as her mother had done. Judith reluctantly did as her father willed and worked as a substitute teacher in various towns until 1965.

Marion, aware of her daughters' dislike for teaching, called one day to tell her about an ad in the newspaper. Belknap College was hiring a secretary for their Director of Admissions. Judith applied and got the job. Free from teaching, she started taking shorthand, typing letters, and running a room-sized IBM computer that typed automatic acceptance (or not) letters to prospective students. When Mr. Erickson, the Director, left for another career, David Walter was hired to replace him. Destiny was at hand as Judith got to know her new boss.

(left, top) Robert Morgan Berry (1911-1997); Marion Josephine Nickles (1911-1997); (bottom) Elverton Berry (1883-1952); Marion Berry with 1st-8th grades in one room school house, North Sandwich (above) Judy, 1947 at Parsonage in Center Sandwich, David Walter's Belknap College ID Badge, Marion (Judy's mother) with Judy 1946

David's story, quite different than Judith's, begins in Massachusetts. His parents, Margaret Harrison Davis (1906-2002) and Carl Waldemar Walter (1905-1992), were both born and raised in Cleveland, OH. They both attended West High School where Carl was on the track team and Margaret was a member of The Castalian Literary Club. They dated all through high school, and graduated together in 1924.

Upon graduation, Carl accepted a scholarship to Harvard College and moved to Cambridge that fall. In 1928, he began his studies to become a doctor at Harvard Medical School. Margaret stayed in Cleveland and attended a five-year nursing program at Western Reserve University Frances Payne Bolton School of Nursing. Following her graduation in 1929, Carl and Margaret were married on September 9th. Ultimately, in 1944, they settled in Holliston, Massachusetts where David and his siblings grew up.

Carl was a formidable man. Graduating from Harvard in 1932, he taught at Harvard Medical School from the 1940s until his retirement in 1972 as Clinical Professor of Surgery. Early in his career, Carl was involved in two incidents that changed his life. First, he witnessed a patient receive a failed blood transfusion, causing blood to spurt all over the operating room. Second, he was asked to investigate what caused the death of five patients after surgery. His research revealed surgical instruments that were not sterile and were infecting patients. This set him on a lifelong quest to discover sterilization techniques.

Wilfred Turenne, a friend of Carl's, developed a temperature control mechanism for use in irons. Carl recognized its potential for use in sterilization. In the mid 1930's, Walter and Turenne obtained the backing of Tom Fenn and Fenwal, Inc. Their company has produced thermostats for use in autoclaves, in-home use, and even for NASA spacecraft. Other companies sprang up from the original: Fenwal Electronics, Fenwal Laboratories, and Fenwal Controls of Japan.

Carl pushed for better surgical techniques in other areas as well. In 1948, he authored *The Aseptic Treatment of Wounds*. He later wrote and produced movies on hospital cleanliness; *I Dress the Wound*, being one. During the 1950s, he also helped to develop the first artificial kidney.

As surgical professor, he taught third-year students the proper way to use instruments. His fanaticism for operating room cleanliness won him many awards and some disgruntled students. He would have the students cover their hands and forearms with lamp black before they scrubbed for surgery. Many were chagrined to discover that their hand washing technique did not remove the black soot. In 1955, he founded the Environmental Sepsis Laboratory at the Peter Bent Brigham Hospital. This group studied the cause of hospital infections by tracking the germs to their source.

In 1934, he started the first blood bank in Boston, one of the first of its kind in the world. He worked on methods to make transfusions safe and the storage of blood practical. In

(above) David Walter as a Cub Scout, 7 years old; 1948 (right) Margaret Walter (1906-2002) and Carl Waldemar Walter (1905-1992) on their 50th wedding anniversary, Back row: Susie Walter, Marty Walter, Carl E.Walter, David Walter, Alice Walter. Middle row: Ruth Helmuth holding Ann, Grandma Leda Walter, George Walter, Grandpa Carl F. Walter Bottom row: Virginia Walter, Tim Walter, MJ Walter, Linda Walter

1947, he completed work on the airless plastic blood bag. It was used in battle for the first time during the Korean War. He was awarded a silver medal from the American Society of Mechanical Engineers. This blood bag is essentially the same blood bag that we are used to seeing today and is the forerunner to intravenous bags used in hospitals worldwide.

On April 28, 1984, Carl was honored by Harvard Medical School for his accomplishments. In 1986, he was awarded a Harvard medal for his life's work and in 1988, a portrait of Carl was dedicated at the Medical School in the auditorium named for him.

It's true the Walters were serious and hardworking, yet of all the things they are remembered for, throwing parties must be near the top of the list. Margaret liked to have fun and used the calendar to her benefit. Every month there was a reason to celebrate, even if was just birthdays. February brought a big, decorated Valentine's box to be opened after dinner. In March, there was corned beef and cabbage for St. Patrick's Day. April brought Easter, and on May 1st, Margaret would hang small baskets filled with flowers on bedroom door knobs in the morning. Christmas was over-the-top, with an impressive Christmas tree, hundreds of holiday cookies, stollen bread, and a wealth of festively wrapped presents.

Legend has it, at one of their annual summer lobster/clambake parties in 1951, the family gathered for a photo. Guests strolled along the gardens, drink in hand, storytelling and laughing. The five-acre, well-tended property brimmed with Roses, Iris, Gladiola, Hollyhocks, and Peonies. A large hedge bordered the west side of the yard. The six children: Carl, Margaret, David, Alice, Linda, and Margaret Jane, posed for their photo. Just as the cameraman was about to snap the shutter, David discreetly slipped a half dollar coin out of his pocket and over his right eyelid. The moment, captured with coin monocle in place, was the start of David's self-made tradition for all subsequent family photos.

Being part of this privileged and educated family, David cultivated a love for science and math. He was sent to study at Fay School in Southborough, Massachusetts and then on to Westminster High School in Connecticut. Inspired by physics, David wanted to design and build nuclear power plants. He attended Case Western Reserve for a year and then transferred to Belknap College in Center Harbor, New Hampshire to finish college. He received a Master's degree in physics and math under Dr. Frye, a retired MIT professor.

David was intelligent, logical, innovative, and willing to take risks. Frustrated by the unresolved problem of nuclear waste, he left the field of engineering and chose to remain at Belknap College as Director of Admissions. It was here he met Judith. David's aptitude for seeing the big picture and ineffable sense for business, later combined with Judith's passion, were destined for the woods of Mason, where a more heart-centered lifestyle focused his math and physics skills toward a greater purpose.

Butter Herbed Baked Fish

¼ Cup Grated parmesan cheese
½ cup butter
²/₃ cup crushed saltine crackers
½ tsp Basil, dried
½ tsp Oregano, dried
½ tsp salt, if desired
¼ tsp Garlic powder
1 pound Sole

In a 9"x13" baking pan, melt the butter in preheated oven. Meanwhile, combine the cracker crumbs, parmesan cheese, basil, oregano, salt, and garlic. Dip the fish filet in the butter, then in the crumb mixture. Arrange the fillets in the baking dish. Bake at 350º for 30 minutes or until the fish is tender.

Cardamon Bars

½ cup butter
½ cup brown sugar
1 tsp salt
1 cup flour
1 tsp ground cardamon seed

Stir together the butter, sugar, and salt. Blend in the flour and the cardamon. Spread mixture in an 8"x12" pan. Bake at 325⁰ for 15 minutes.

Spread with the following mixture:
2 eggs, well beaten
1 cup brown sugar
1 tsp vanilla
2 TBS flour
1/2 tsp baking powder
1 ½ cups shredded coconut
1 cup chopped walnuts

Add the sugar and vanilla to eggs and beat until thick and foamy. Add remaining ingredients. Mix well and spread over the baked mixture. Return to oven and bake at 325⁰ for 25 minutes. Cool and cut into bars.

Photo by Brian Woodbury

The Walter's relationship evolved from co-workers, to romance, and finally marriage in 1966. David built a house on the shore of Lake Winnipesaukee and there they started their family with Judith's daughter Shelly (Age 3) from a previous marriage. A picture window in the living room provided a lake view and nature entertained. The deep snow melted into the mud of spring. Tadpoles transformed into frogs and loons called in the summer. When Autumn crept in, the green woods released their red, orange, and yellow leaves in surrender to winter's song of slumber.

Life on the lake was constantly changing, along with the Walter household, with the addition of three more children. Four years drifted by, Christmas arrived again and with it the frenzy of wrapping paper, boxes, and bows. Andrew, not quite a year old, amused himself in his playpen. Michael, at two-years-old, was kept entertained by his older sisters Wendy and Shelly. Judy sat to rest from cooking and cleaning with one of her gifts, *Take Joy*, a book by Tasha Tudor.

Turning the pages sent goosebumps up and down her arms. Her stomach clenched and her eyes widened. *I am so inspired*, she thought. Tudor's simple illustrations, back-to-the-land lifestyle, old fashioned dress, dedication to gardening, and love of celebration resonated deeply. It felt as if she had been waiting for this moment. She was just twenty-seven; naïve, yet willing and creative, longing to fulfill a purpose. She knew in that instant what her path would be and she loved Ms. Tudor for awakening it. She savored each page, enjoying the legends the most.

Judith determined to make a plan, but with children and a household to manage, her dream of crafting and selling her wares would have to wait. It wasn't until two years later, when she and David, tired of living in a resort area, decided to move. They wanted more land and to be free of commercial development. David searched for a job and was hired as a purchasing agent by Union Twist Drill in Athol, Massachusetts. They moved to New Ipswich, New Hampshire in 1972 where the aspiration for a more self-sufficient lifestyle had its beginnings on Willard Road, with a pony, chickens, a St. Bernard named Bingo, and a vegetable garden.

The new job consumed David's time, leaving Judith with the daily drudgery of household duties. She searched for work, trying newspaper writing, nursery school teaching, and substituting at the local high school, with little satisfaction. Her desire to make a living through gardening, collecting antiques, and working on craft projects nagged at her constantly. She came to realize that a life not led by imagination can be empty, cold and dark like infertile soil, so she allowed herself to dream.

Judith and David kept searching for the perfect location to start their dream of a farm and gift shop. And on that fateful evening in 1974, when traveling up the long dirt driveway, they found the answer. Their "Pickity" adventures in the woods of Mason, New Hampshire were about to begin. Without having a clue about running a business, the choice was made. Bravely, they crossed the threshold, venturing into the unknown and open to whatever would come.

(above) David and Judy. Wedding Day, July 10th 1966, Center Harbor NH; 1972 Andrew and pony 'Blacky' Willard Rd, New Ipswich 1972; Shelly with St Bernard 'Bingo' Willard Rd, New Ipswich; What we called 'The White House' built in 1810, Willard Rd, New Ipswich

January

The Pickity Shed circa 1979

Epiphany, or "Little Christmas", is the time when the wise men arrived in Bethlehem to pay homage to the holy child. In parts of rural England, ancient farm festivals have combined with Christian symbolism. Cider is poured around the roots of fruit trees, and cider soaked cakes are placed in the branches. A song is sung to the trees – "hats full, caps full, three – score baskets full, and all our pockets full too." This is called "wassailing the trees" to assure the triumph of the coming warm spring over the current cold-weather.

Janus, in Roman mythology, was a God who had two faces, one which looked into the past and the other into the future. Janus served as the god of gates and doors. His name comes from the Latin Janua, meaning gate. January, first month of the year, was named for Janus. The turn of the year is the time for omens and superstitions; turning away from the old year and facing the new. The first person to cross the threshold on New Year's Day indicates the sort of fortune the household may expect in the coming year.

The ancient and pagan figure of Old Father Time, complete with sickle and the sands of time running out, traditionally represents the dying year. The sentiment of "Auld Lang Syne" is in tune with the ancient belief that at the New Year ancestors return to the family hearth.

January's sun is weak, and icicles hang from the roof, many of them three- feet- long! We will use some of these for freezing homemade ice cream. Snow is piling up and the red Jeep with its plow is getting its exercise.

Temperatures plunge to zero and below, and we hope the tender roots and the Earth are warm enough. When a warmer day is forecast, we sneak out for a day of skiing. Holiday decorations have been packed away for another year, and in the dining room, silver stars hang in the windows. Framed woodcut prints embellish the walls, and on the mantle, champagne glasses are bubbled over with "frothy" ribbons.

This is our first time for rest after many busy months, and we take full advantage!

Walter, Judy (1984) *The Pickity Place Cookbook,* Mason, NH
Herb Farm Press

Winter in the 80's when it snowed so much we could sled off the shop roof!

Although the month of February is still chill with winter's cold, it promises the spring to come. Rejoice in the season of love! The old-fashioned Valentine includes many meaningful symbols. The ribbon and lace frills are associated with the days of knighthood when a man in armor wore a ribbon given him by his lady love. Cupid is one of the gods of mythology, whose Latin name means desire. The Rose is the most loved flower the world over, and if rearranged, the letters spell "Eros" the God of love. The doves are birds which mate for life, thus symbolizing fidelity.

Symbols of love include the love knot. The two circles intertwined, side-by-side, represent affection without beginning and without end. When it is fashioned from gold, it signifies eternal love.

Many foods are thought to stimulate affection; these "foods of love" include various meats, fish, fruits, and wines. Fruits that have seeds are considered important foods of love. The apple has been associated with love since the Garden of Eden.

There are certain herbs that are thought to cool and quiet the emotions. These include Fennel, Chicory, and Rue. Southernwood is known as the passion herb. It is also known by two other names: "Lads Love" and "Maiden's Ruin".

Seed catalogs have started arriving and we are dreaming and planning ahead. Lists are made and remade, and ideas for new gardens begin to unfold in our thoughts. We take inventory in the greenhouse, and plan for the thousands of new seedlings soon to appear. Winter birds fly in and out of feeders, and the gray squirrel tries in vain to steal some of their bounty!

A Valentine box, decorated with lace and red hearts, sits on the old Parsons bench, and Victorian cards with scenes of love grace the mantle. A friend has brought us a beautiful, heart-shaped wreath fashioned from Heather. We heap on more wood, sip a cup of steaming spice tea, and think about ideas for new herbal products. We explore the markets, looking for new and exciting things to offer our customers. "If winter comes, can spring be far behind?" (Percy Bysshe Shelley)

Walter, Judy (1984) *The Pickity Place Cookbook*, Mason, NH
Herb Farm Press

March

Our menu for March begins with Curry Cheese spread, served with crackers.

To celebrate the feast day of St. Patrick we have chosen a hearty Potato soup seasoned with white pepper and papricka.

Maple syrup gathered from our own trees sweetens the ginger maple bread.

Enjoy the colorful tossed salad with dill weed dressing. We've added calendula petals which, we are told, are beneficial to the disposition and helpful to conversation.

For the main course, choose:

* Spanokopita ~ pastry triangles filled with spinach and feta cheese and seasoned with oregano.

OR

* Irish Brown Stew ~ actually a tasty casserole dish with a hint of lovage.

Both served with green bean bundles.

For dessert: Grasshopper Crepes

To drink: Lemon or Spice tea
Cinnamon Coffee.

Spring circa 1979

The March winds have arrived - time to savor some of the first delights of spring! Sap flows in the trees, the first pussy willows appear, and hibernating animals leave their winter sleeping places.

There are many superstitions about March. We often hear that "March comes in like a lion and goes out like a lamb". March was the first month on the ancient Roman calendar. Its name honors Mars, the Roman God of war. The early farmers referred to the first three days of March as unlucky. If rain fell on one of these days, a poor crop was foretold. Take heed and do not plant seed until March 4!

The vernal equinox takes place on March 20 or 21st and marks the beginning of spring. It is a time when the sun is directly over the equator and day and night are nearly equal all over the earth.

Early spring in New Hampshire begins the sapping season. Cold nights and warm days start the sap flowing in the sugar maples. Did you know? It takes from 35 to 45 gallons of sap to make one gallon of maple syrup!

Although we know winter is not yet over, a spring thaw has made the road muddy and our fingers itch to feel the earth again.

The first pussy willows are showing off their fuzzy backs, and a few brave Snowdrops are blooming in the snow. Soon we will be shearing the sheep, and they will look naked without their warm, woolly, winter coats. Snow has disappeared in some protected spots, and the Egyptian onions and a few other bold plants are poking their heads above the ground.

The Forsythia bushes are loaded with fat buds, and we bring a branch into the warm house to force the blossoms open. In the greenhouse, Crocuses and Daffodils are opening, and soon we will have Tulips in full bloom.

The magic of the plant cycle has begun, and trays of minute seedlings are everywhere! We watch and rejoice as they mature and become useful for fragrance, medicine, and for flavoring.

Walter, Judy (1984) *The Pickity Place Cookbook,* Mason, NH
Herb Farm Press

Photos circa 1940

The front door and carriage house which is now the main shop.

Side view of the house through the woods. The black door became the entrance to the restaurant.

Large lilac shrub you would have seen coming down the driveway.

The old greenhouse and patio with the carriage house in the background.

The black door is now white. An arbor has been added on the left.

The lilacs are replaced by a cherry tree.

Front gardens before an arbor was added to the carriage house.

View from the driveway.

Arbor now added to the carriage house.

Great view of the driveway into the carriage house.

Laundry drying in the carriage house. A lot of trees and growth before the gardens.

Front of house with carriage shed.

The garden shed with view of the mountains in the background!
The trough in front left corner would have been filled with water for horses.
The grape arbor has been built behind and to the left of the shed.

Side view of the house before the arbor.

Coming down the driveway before the gardens.

Some kind of celebration in the front yard.
(Black front door and white window trim)

Here you can see the slate patio and arbor clearly.

The front door and greenhouse to the left. There is a large stone in the driveway (shown between the door and windows) perhaps used as a hitching post for the horses.

On the side of the front lawn. The driveway is on the other side of the fence.

Working the lawn long before there were any gardens.

The greenhouse and front door before there were bricks or raised garden beds.

Front lawn.

The front of the house before the addition of a greenhouse.

The water trough and lovely view of lawn in front of the arbor off the carriage house.

Sprouting

"In this fast- paced world, it is too frequently the case that people accept what society, family members and the authorities, whom nobody ever seems to question, believe regarding how to live their lives. And yet, the happiest people I know have been those who have accepted the primary responsibility for their own spiritual and physical well-being - those who have inner strength, courage, determination, common sense and faith in the process of creating more balanced and satisfying lives for themselves."

Ann Wigmore

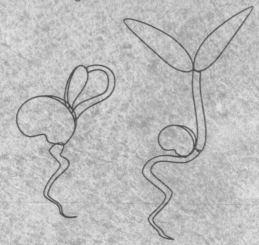

Why the name "Pickity Place"? It is one of those made-up words that springs from the imagination when you are having fun. "The Picks" bubbled up spontaneously as a nickname. Anything David and Judith, or Mr. and Mrs. Pick, liked with a certain sensibility became "Pickity." The house David built in Kranewood Shores of Moultonborough, was the original "Pickity Place". Over the years, the name has been misheard as, "Rickety Place", "Pickity Patch" or "Picket Fence", among others.

So The 'Picks' married and moved to Nutting Hill Road, ready to begin their farm. Six months passed, when one day they received a surprisingly serendipitous phone call. Bobbi Macozek, an old friend living in Maine, offered to sell her herb gardens, copies of all her herbal recipes, craft ideas, and various jars and props, including the winnower (an old-fashioned tool that cracks and discards grain husks) that now resides in the drying shed, all priced at a whopping six hundred dollars. Her irresistible offer was accepted and the Pickity shop had its beginnings.

Bobbi's gardens were dug up in one trip and transplanted into raised bed boxes David built behind the carriage house (what would later become the gift shop). Southernwood, Oregano, various Mints, Chinese Daisies, Thyme, Chives, Wormwood, Artemisia, Yarrow, and Mugwort settled in.

Having little knowledge of herbs at the time, Judy studied voraciously to familiarize herself with herbal remedies and their mystical qualities. Her keen memory for smells guided and taught her more than anything else.

After planting the garden beds, it was time to configure the original Pickity shop, comprised of one room the first year. Converted from a carriage shed of three or four 'horse stalls', the shop was a rustic old barn, with a time-worn creaky floor. The five ancient windows were dressed up with bright yellow curtains and an old but colorful oriental runner rug covered the floorboards. A woodstove radiated the only source of heat. An antique wooden cash register discovered by a good friend was built into the checkout counter. This wooden drawer became a bone of contention for years, as Judith was adamant computers were not to be used in the shop...EVER... in order to maintain an old-fashioned esthetic. David built tables and shelves around the room and Judith covered them in burlap and colorful fabrics. Many antique cupboards and racks discovered by Judith were incorporated to display herbal wares, candles, ribbon, and unique gifts. Wild herbs and flowers hung from the rafters and from old wagon wheels suspended from the ceiling. Pungent scents filled the room and a corner was dedicated to the children's crafts.

The Walters of Pickity Place
Krainewood Shores, Center Harbor, N.H.

Sign at the end of the driveway; The Walter's original Pickity Place stationary;
The original Pickity Place house in Moultonborough.

PICKITY PLACE
MASON, N.H. 03048

Two years from purchase, Pickity Place had its official open house on April 19th, 1976. The remote location called for postcard invitations sent to as many friends, relatives, and neighbors that could be thought of (as well as all the members of the Souhegan Country Club where David and Judith were members). But it almost didn't happen.

Several days before the grand opening, the family was playing cards at the kitchen table. Seven-year-old Andrew wandered in from the shop, and in his unperturbed, quiet way said, "Dad, should there be flames coming up from behind the shop stove?" David ran to find the back wall of the shop in flames while Judith hailed the fire department. David flung water at the wall from the iron tea kettle on the stove and managed to douse the flame. The fire department arrived after the fact, bounding in with axes to make sure no inside walls were hazardous. No more hot spots were found and minimal damage was done. As a result, a firewall was put up behind the wood stove. Lesson learned!!

Andrew, the official hero of the day, was promised a reward – a gift of his choice. He selected a camper's jack-knife at the local hardware store, one he would have to grow into and would later come in handy for carving. Andrew liked to work with wood. One of his first contributions to the 'kid's corner' in the shop were wooden moon faces, cut with a jigsaw. They were about 5" high, painted yellow, with a string for hanging and at a price of fifty cents! Judith still has one hanging in her kitchen. To this day, Andrew can make most anything with wood and is handy with carpentry, electricity, plumbing, and anything else that requires putting things together and getting them to work.

The open house was on! Judith and her friends, Chris Arnold and Carolyn Thomas, dressed in long country dresses and stood ready to serve refreshments and show off the wares. The children were ready and hopeful with a popcorn stand, while the dog was rushing about with excitement.

Almost all the treasures were handmade by the family and local crafts-people: herbal wreaths, sachets in various shapes and fabrics, herbal vinegar, dips and spreads, mulled cider, and herbal blends for flavoring meats and fish, to name a few. Sections of the shop were designated for cooking herbs, fragrant herbs, essential oils, and herbal teas. There were soaps in beautiful wrappings, mortar and pestles, and kitchen gadgets. Local crafters provided scented hot pads, wooden toys, and exquisite handmade dolls. Rolls of fabric and ribbon were added to sell by the yard, as well as herbal books, greeting cards, and posters by the well-known woodcut artist Mary Azarian. People came! They were curious to see what this 'Pickity Place' was all about. How could anyone imagine a shop in such a remote location?

The grand opening was a success and spurred the dream of a business into reality. Over the next year, so many people visited that more roaming space was needed. David, Michael, and Andrew went to work to expand the gardens by clearing the back path abutting the neighbors. It would later get filled-in with gravel as a road. A long hedge of Lavender was cultivated as a stunning border. Years later, lettuce and tomatoes along with a 'cutting garden' for edible flowers like Calendula, Viola, and Borage were grown for use in the restaurant.

(left) The postcard invitation to the open house; The winnower in the drying shed; Advertisement in *Yankee* magazine in the 70's.; (above) left to right: Judith at the shop door; The hedge of lavender along the back road; David in the shop circa 1976; Middle left to right: The start of the flower beds in front of the shop circa 1976; Wooden moon made by Andrew; The wood stove used for display in the summer; Bottom left to right: The shop goodies; the shop circa 1976; David, Michael and Andrew building the addition to the shop 1980.

31

"Being Pickity" not only included crafting and gardening, but tending to a family of animals. David built a shiplap barn with a hay loft in 1979 to replace one that had blown down in the Hurricane of 1938. It was meant to house their

other family members: pigs, chickens, geese, sheep, horses (Tippy and Chief), a pony named Mitsy, two steers (Basil and Ginger), a crazy Irish Setter named Duncan, and many cats. Some customers may remember "Spotty" the cat, who lived for over eighteen years. Another of the many cats snuck onto a UPS truck, took a nice tour of Mason, and was eventually delivered home. The barn also provided uncountable hours for the children to build haybale forts and play to their heart's content.

The gift shop's popularity grew enough to inspire an addition in 1980. A variety of new handmade goodies, including space for their signature packaged dried herbs and a new Glenwood wood burning cook stove, were added.

While the shop grew, so did the children. They trekked daily to the school bus stop, on what they would call, 'the short or long paths'; short-cuts through the woods to Nutting Hill Road. The little brick schoolhouse in Mason and Appleton School in New Ipswich their destination. At the end of the day, they would hike back through what became their second home; the extraordinary woods. A strong sense of connection and presence was discovered there. They could certainly imagine Little Red Riding Hood skipping along those paths to Grandmother's house, especially since they were emulating her journey. Thankfully, they never met a wolf.

Waldorf education came on the scene for the family in 1979. Andrew, Michael, and Wendy left the public school system for High Mowing and Pine Hill schools, who are now known as one entity, on Abbott Hill in Wilton. At that time, Pine Hill was located in Old Wilton Center for grades 1-6, while High Mowing the high school, also housed the seventh and eighth graders in the library building.

Developed by Rudolf Steiner in 1919 in Germany, Waldorf Education aspires to educate the whole child, including the heart, hands, and head. It attracted the Walters, as it embodied the back to nature esthetic, self-reliant living, and creativity the family already aspired to. Michael and Andrew learned how to knit, sew, paint, and felt, while Wendy learned the skill of throwing production pottery. Mrs. Isobel Karl, her wise and witty teacher, also taught other well-known potters such as Guy Wolf (of Guy Wolf Pottery, Bantam CT), Pamela Owens (of Jugtown Pottery, Seagrove NC), and Sharry Stevens-Grunden (of SRS-Grunden Pottery Oak Bluffs, MA), but that's another book! Mrs. Karl is still teaching as of this writing at the spritely age of 94!

The creative spirit of the family renewed the property. The cycle of the seasons guided their tasks as the success of "Being Pickity" grew out of a sacred and celebratory Spirit. Judith found great solace in expressing herself through the festivals. They were something tangible for her to dig into and gave each year more meaning and purpose. In addition, the family's creativity, growth, and interests were directly reflected back in the shop, gardens, and animals. They were Pickity Place and it was them. It 'worked' on them as they worked on it. It was no longer a dream, but a lifestyle.

(left) The Ash Tree, one of the oldest in NH; (above) Cat-Pussy Willow; Cat-Spotty; Daughter Shelly on horse Tippy; Sheep-Angelica and Rosemary; Dog-Duncan; David with Duncan; The Geese-Heath, Heather, Holly and Hyssop; Steer-Basil.

Tulips outside the old greenhouse which was rebuilt in 1998.

April

Many of the customs connected with Easter come from pagan festivals of spring. In most countries, Easter comes in early spring, when green grass and warm sunshine begin to push away the ice and snow of winter. The name Easter perhaps comes from Eoster, a Teutonic goddess of spring.

In ancient Europe, the rabbit symbolizes birth and life and was considered a symbol of the moon. Perhaps it became an Easter symbol because the moon determines the date of Easter.

As a prelude to Easter, Germans celebrate Shrove Tuesday and eat fastnachts and pretzels. In Great Britain, it is the custom to eat Carling's, or peas, on Carling Sunday, the fifth Sunday of Lent. Hot cross buns, with their cross shaped topping, have ties which extend back to pre-Christian times when the cross represented both Sun and fire.

Early Mesopotamian Christians were the first to use colored eggs for Easter, and red dye was used to represent the joy of the resurrection. Food is often decorated with the letters XB for "Christos Voskres" (Christ is risen).

April arrives and the frost is leaving the ground. The weather teases us and the changing temperature heaves the plants and lifts them to the elements. We hasten to tamp down their roots to protect them from still frosty nights.

The Bloodroot is coming in the dye garden, and the Coltsfoot will be next, with its Dandelion-like flowers. We look forward to the first tender green Lovage leaves – we will brew these into a spring tonic as the early countrywomen did.

We build-in a natural protection for our plants by interplanting fragrant herbs, flowers, and vegetables. Strong scents confuse, thus repelling invading insects.

Tiny seedlings dropped from last year's harvest appear in unlikely spots and tilling must wait until we move them to their proper homes.

Spring has put excitement in our hearts and winter woes are forgotten!

Walter, Judy (1984) *The Pickity Place Cookbook*, Mason, NH Herb Farm Press

May

Mayday, the favorite festival of spring, brings us marvelous customs, costumes, decorations, dances, and foods to signal the changing season.

During medieval times, Maypoles were the center of the revelry, splendid with their crowns of ribbon and streamers, and decorations of flowers. Dancers with bells on their ankles and wrists stamp the ground to awaken it. May bells were rung to alert the sleeping fields and forests to the time of rebirth, and May baskets were hung on the doors.

Spring green foods were served in abundance and always included a cookie man called "Jack and the Bush", for on his head, he wore a wreath of green.

During ancient Celtic rights, the queen of May directed the games of competition.

Sweet Woodruff, the very essence of spring with its vibrant green leaves and early blossoms, was steeped in Rhine wine to make the German Maribowl. The plant's German name – Waldmeister – means "master of the woods".

Traditionally, a bit of Bangkok (oatmeal) cake was served and thrown to the witches, who must wait for their portion of the feast.

Sunny May mornings force us early from our beds for a trip to the gardens, and we are all pleased that our spring efforts have begun to reward us with an abundance of fresh herbs for cooking. Borders of Chives already need clipping and the salad Burnet, with its cucumber flavor, is ready for picking.

The cats have discovered the first tender growth of the Catnip and are sleeping it off in the sundrenched wheelbarrow! Huge pots of Rosemary, Sweet Bay, and the tender Lavenders are moved outside for their summer vacation. It is time to air the drying shed, to remove the remaining remnants of last year's harvest, and ready it for the new crop. Sprigs of sweet Woodruff are picked for the luncheon tables and we bring out the cool-looking blue tablecloths for the summer months.

As we take a walk along the path in the woods, we breathe in the earthy scents of new life.

Walter, Judy (1984) *The Pickity Place Cookbook*, Mason, NH
Herb Farm Press

The May pole in the back yard circa 1980.

June

In the old Latin calendar, June was the fourth month and had 29 days. Its name originally denoted the month in which crops grew to ripeness.

Midsummer Eve was a merry time of mixing customs of ancient sun worship with medieval Christian lore. Cuckoo-foot ale was a highlight of the Midsummer feast. It was spiced with Ginger, Anise, and Basil, and celebrated the cuckoo bird; whose song is a sure proof of the summer season.

In the 16th century, it was the custom for nearly every village in Germany to have a bonfire on the eve of St. John; June 23. Perhaps the ancient peoples built their fires to hold their warmth in the heavens as the summer solstice approached.

St. John's Eve was also the time when the magic Fernseed was gathered to render one invisible, and crowns of Mugwort were worn.

Walter, Judy (1984) *The Pickity Place Cookbook,* Mason, NH Herb Farm Press

Lovage Dip

Chill 3 hard-boiled eggs, then chop them very fine. Combine with ½ cup chopped fresh Lovage leaves, ¼ cup of minced Parsley, and a sprig of minced Tarragon. Add the above to one cup of cottage cheese. Mix well and add 1 cup of sour cream. Add pepper to taste. Chill to blend flavors.

Photo by Brian Woodbury

Maibowie
(May Wine)

1 Small Bunch Sweet Woodruff
1 Bottle Moselle or Rhine Wine
2 TBS Sugar
2/3 Cup Water
1 pint fresh Strawberries

Remove damaged leaves from the Woodruff and put the whole bunch, including flowers, into a tall glass jug. Pour over the wine. Gently heat the sugar and water in a pan and add to the wine. Cover loosely and chill. When serving add fresh strawberry slices.

Photo by Brian Woodbury

Photo by Brian Woodbury

Spinach Basil quiche

1 Baked 9" pastry shell
1 12 oz. package frozen chopped spinach, thawed
1 TBS butter
1/3 cup chopped onion
3/4 cup half and half
2 large eggs
1/8 tsp ground black pepper
1 8 oz. container ricotta cheese
1 tsp fresh basil, chopped
nutmeg

Drain the thawed spinach, pressing out all liquid. Melt the butter in a small skillet. Add the onion and cook for three minutes. Add the half and half and heat only until scalded. In a medium bowl, beat the eggs with the basil and pepper. Add the ricotta and beat until blended. Add the hot half and half and spinach and mix well. Pour into the baked shell. Sprinkle freshly grated nutmeg on top. Bake at 425° for about 35 minutes. Cool to lukewarm before cutting.

Crispy Rosemary Potatoes

2 Large Baking Potatoes, peeled
¼ cup butter, melted
Black pepper
6 sprigs Rosemary, finely snipped

Preheat oven to 350º. Slice the potatoes ½" thick and quarter the slices. Place in a single layer on a baking sheet and brush with ½ the melted butter. Sprinkle with ½ the Rosemary and pepper. Bake until golden, about 15 minutes. Turn the slices over, brush with remaining butter, then sprinkle with remaining rosemary. Bake till crisp and golden, about 15 more minutes. Serve immediately.

Green Beans with Savory

1 lb. green beans
2 tsp fresh Savory, chopped
4 TBS sour cream
2 tsp Egyptian Onion stalk, chopped

Cook the beans till tender. Drain. Add the Savory, onions, and sour cream. Cover and heat gently. Serve hot.

Onion Tarragon Pie

Pastry to line a 9" pie pan
1 cup onions, finely sliced
2 TBS butter
¼ cup cheddar cheese grated
3 Eggs, slightly beaten
1 ½ TBS flour
½ cup milk
2 tsp prepared mustard
2 TBS fresh Tarragon, chopped
1 can golden mushroom soup

Sauté the onions in the butter. Line the pie pan with the pastry and place the onions on the pie shell. Sprinkle with the grated cheese. Blend together the eggs, flour, milk, mustard, Tarragon, and soup to pour over the onions and cheese. Bake at 350º for 45 minutes or until set.

Photo by Brian Woodbury

Growing

Before the reward there must be labor.
You plant before you harvest.
You sow in tears before you reap joy.

Ralph Ransom

"And the day came when the risk to remain
tight in a bud was more painful than the
risk it took to blossom."

Anais Nin

"If you're green you grow, if you're ripe you rot," David explained to a local reporter. The journalists came often, hoping to uncover the mystery of these 'Pickity beings' and their unusual success in the far reaches of the woods, disproving the well-known real estate phrase 'location, location, location'. Not one for interviews, David did his best. Neither Judith or David enjoyed being the center of attention, but they told their story time and time again to clarify who they were, what they did, and why.

What the newspaper writers didn't learn was that it was David who took on expanding the business. A problem solver and creative thinker, he was the cornerstone for financial success. A practical New Englander, adept at using what he had at hand, he knew how to utilize the property to its fullest potential to generate different streams of income. His overarching vision, up against Judith's pragmatism, could cause friction on occasion, calling them to review what it meant to be "Pickity".

Meher Baba captures the transformation of Pickity Place in his assertion that, "to penetrate into the essence of all being and significance and to release the fragrance of that inner attainment for the benefit and guidance of others by expressing in the world of forms, truth, love, purity, and beauty – this is the sole game which has any intrinsic and absolute worth."[3]

This metamorphosis was spurred on by two major changes. First, the original Pickity barn was converted into a gift shop and greenhouse in 1981. Shortly thereafter, the family's home was transformed into Grandmother's Room and Teahouse. Customer demand drove both.

Many people at that time were embracing the world of herbs and growing their own gardens. Initially, Pickity had space to display a couple dozen plants in a humble farm wagon until it became clear more space was needed. The addition of the 36x48 hoop greenhouse provided enough room for *three hundred* types of annuals and perennials. A portion of the adjacent barn was converted into a gardening shop with gifts like bird houses, spoon wind chimes, garden tools, and seeds.

The Pickity 'tea house' was also inspired by customers, who after the long drive to the shop, would ask, "where can we find lunch?" In those days, Nutting Hill Road was uninhabited and surrounding towns did not have many restaurants. The combination of "Tea House and Grandmother's Room" met their needs.

"Grandmother's Room" (David and Judith's bedroom), and "Little Red Riding Hood Museum" (previously a library sitting area) a check-in place for reservations and gift shop, were designed to replicate Elizabeth Orton Jones (1910-2005) book *Little Red Riding Hood*. Stencils were commissioned from Merilyn Markham and a bedspread was hand-stitched by Andrea Fox to bring Jones' book illustrations to life. A papier mache wolf head made by daughter Wendy and friend Gina Daniello was professionally painted by Diane Tigue from New Ipswich and tucked into the bed. David and Judith slept in "Grandmother's" bed each night, returning the "wolf head" in the morning.

Paper Mache Wolf Head made by Wendy Walter and friend Gina Daniello; Signage outside The Grandmother's Room; Judith, Andrew and David cooking in the 80's; Pickity Place pottery made by Wendy at High mowing School in the 80's.

Jones, a revered member of Mason, was published by Golden Books from 1948 -1979. "Twig", the locals nicknamed her (after her book *Twig* was published), purchased a house in Mason after a visit on a business trip in 1945. The house which was "up for taxes", was acquired with her first royalty check of $2000.

Jones grew up in Highland Park, Illinois, with her father George Robert Jones, her mother Jessie May Orton, and a younger brother and sister. Her first book, *Ragman of Paris and his Ragamuffins* was based on her experiences in France. She was a student at Ecole des Beaux Arts in Fontainebleau and the Academie Colarossi.

Jones won the Caldecott Medal in 1945 in recognition of her book *Prayer for a Child*. The medal, named in honor of nineteenth-century English illustrator Randolph Caldecott, is awarded annually to the artist of the most distinguished American picture book for children. When asked why Jones decided to become an artist, she answered, "But you don't decide to become an artist, you just are."[4]

Her version of *Little Red Riding Hood* resulted from the pursuit of Lucille Olge, editor of Little Golden Books, during the American Library Association's Annual Conference in the 1940s. Each morning of the conference, Jones enjoyed breakfast at the upscale Waldorf-Astoria and found a surprise note on a silver breakfast tray. Charmed by the editor's compliments and persistence, Jones agreed to meet. By the conference's end, she had signed on to illustrate a Little Golden Book title of her choosing.

Jones loved the wooded paths and large ash tree adjacent to the back entrance of Pickity Place (now the dining room entrance), and decided they were the perfect setting for her book. She used her own home as the model for other illustrations. She once explained, "I pretended Little Red Riding Hood was in my home. She was standing right over there in front of that fireplace" (Boston Globe, 1993).

In the original version of the book (Edition A), Red Riding Hood delivers wine to her grandmother and is portrayed with a tiny glass, also having a sip. Outraged members of The Woman's Christian Temperance Union sent hundreds of letters to Olge in defiance of a young lady drinking wine. Edition B of the book removed the word wine and replaced it with grape juice. Little Red Riding Hood brings her Grandmother "a piece of cake, a pat of butter, and a bottle of grape juice"[5] with the intention of eating together. The book also omitted an illustration of the wolf knocking on the front door as it was deemed

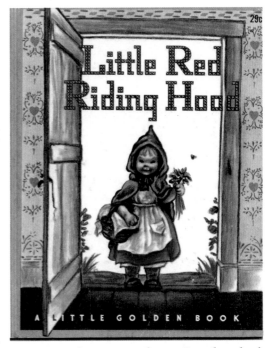

"too scary". The idea of a Pickity "Tea House", was to provide customers with the experience of eating together at Grandmother's house. It took over the family's kitchen, dining room, and living room. The uniquely themed monthly menu, based on the festivals, made it a hit. A five-course herbal luncheon with three seatings a day included crackers, bread with herbal butter, soup, salad, a main course (a choice of vegetarian or meat), and dessert, all for only $8.95!! Children were offered a "Grandmother's Basket" adorned with a red and white checked napkin in honor of Red Riding Hood, containing their choice of sandwich, a piece of fruit, and a cookie. The hand-written and decorated menus always included a story about the festival of the month and the herbs that went along with it.

Left: Elizabeth Orton Jones; The cover illustration of Jones' book *Little Red Riding Hood*;
Right: Illustration of path through the woods on p.6 of Jones' book *Little Red Riding Hood*.

Moth Preventative

Combine equal amounts of
Wormwood
Southernwood
Lavender

Natural Fly Repellent

Combine:
Crumbled Bay Leaves
Crushed whole Cloves
Eucalyptus leaves
Lemon Balm leaves
Place in an open bowl to scent a room.

(above) Illustration of the wolf at the door from Jones' *Little Red Riding Hood* p.16; (right) David's grandparents photos which hung in the dining room: Daisy Miranda Harrison (Davis) 1876-1962 and Charles Ulysses Davis 1872-1950.

The dining room decor was designed to change according to the traditional festivals and holidays. Adelma Grenier Simmons (1903–1997), one of the twentieth century's leading herbal figures in America and owner of Caprilands Herb Farm in Coventry, Connecticut for over fifty-five years, deepened Judith's knowledge of herbal use and customs and inspired many of the monthly changes, such as Mary Azarian woodcuts, swags of Grapevine or Bittersweet, or ribbons with Rosehip adorning the fireplace mantle. A bookshelf in the small dining room displayed decorative china, gourds, corn husk dolls, or an Irish tea set, depending on the festival. A different tablecloth color with a potted herb centerpiece enhanced the monthly transformation. One signature monthly change was the candy accompanying the luncheon check. Throughout the year, candy peas and carrots, candy raspberries, candy corn, or jelly pumpkins were served. Amidst the monthly changes, some things stayed the same. The most important to note were photographs of Daisy and Charles Davis, David's grandparents. Long since passed away, they were displayed reverently on either side of the fireplace in the dining room for more than twenty-five years. Their support was felt, and it was believed their spirits hovered nearby.

Mary Collins (1937-2013), a close friend of Judith's, came monthly for twenty years to help bring the festivals to life. She designed beautiful fresh flower wreaths to hang on the doorways and all the table centerpieces. She had a great eye for detail and a knack for perfection.

As the business changed and grew, challenges came up. David and Judith's conviction had to be strong, vision clear, and will to persevere rooted in deep faith that all would work out. Their business provided a natural framework for learning about economics, people, and survival skills, and as with any new enterprise, Pickity had its glitches.

One of Pickity's first customers was a pretty young woman from California who had seen an ad in the paper. She praised the shop, filled a basket with products, and asked to pay by check for an amount over $100. Thrilled to reap such a large purchase, the check was accepted and promptly returned by the bank due to a lack of funds. It seemed this young lady found her Aunt's old checkbook in the attic and went on a spending spree. There was little recourse for collection so they were stuck with a bounced check and were more than a little discouraged. That was a large 'burn' at the time, but over the course of twenty-five years they had an extremely low rate of bounced checks – perhaps three a year. For the most part, Pickity's revenue did not draw from tourists, but from regular visitors truly interested in herbs and quality hand-made items.

Their first advertisement was placed in *Yankee* magazine for a 'moth bag repellent'. Strangely enough, the Environmental Protection Agency got ahold of the ad and sent a representative to investigate. The EPA was concerned about the potential 'residue' left over from manufacturing and wanted to verify its proper disposal. Who knew a cloth bag filled with a mix of Raspberry Leaf, Cloves, and Orris Root, tied with a ribbon, could cause such distress! David spent hours explaining that only herbs were used and there was NO residue. In the end, they agreed to change the ad to read 'preventative' instead of 'repellent' as a solution.

Before and After

The Walter's living room before it became a dining room.

The large dining room in the 1980's.

The sitting room or library before it became a reception area.

Grandmother's room and Red Riding hood 'museum'.

David and Judith's bedroom before the wolf!

The bedroom decorated to look line Jones' illustration.

The Walter's kitchen before it went commercial.

Enjoying Advent at the table in the kitchen in the early 80's.
Stephanie Arnold, Andrew Walter, David Arnold, Christine Arnold.

The Walter's dining room which would become the small restaurant dining room.

The large dining room looking into the small dining room..

Recipe Testers

Candles lit on the long wobble table;
that red tablecloth
wax stained
from the candles you warned us
not to pick at.
Silverware set for six.

And then the food-
the house would smell
of roast beef boiling in a kettle,
Bay Leaves and Lovage wafting
around, proding the stomach
to make the lips ask, "When's dinner?"
"When's dinner?"

In the summer it was
apple stuffed chicken
or a cool cucumber soup to sip on
at lunch time. Sweets would follow
like sesame seed bars or a pumpkin parfait
each as a test of our taste.

Sometimes served five courses,
each month hoping to find
the Pickity recipe
we would help you decide - we got to
try all the tastes

Wendy Walter,
1991 , The Pickity Place Cookbook Volume III
Herb Farm Press

The hoop greenhouse, shop and barn; Judith in the greenhouse circa 1985; Inside the hoop greenhouse; The greenhouse shop. Left: Judith at the shed door circa 1985; Herbs hanging in the shed; Judith making wreaths in the shed.

Another time, a woman, clearly enjoying her shopping experience, took the liberty of changing price tags on a basket full of products - to her benefit of course. Judith witnessed it all and very graciously blamed her employees for the pricing mistakes by asking the perpetrator, one product at a time, if she wanted to purchase them at the correct price. On another occasion, three thousand dollars robbed from the coffers motivated David to install a security system. The thief broke in through the wolf's bedroom window and was never caught. Well, what goes around comes around. Better watch your back whoever you are!

They never knew what kind of challenges would present themselves. During lunch one day, an elderly man fell face first into his soup. His wife, too embarrassed to do anything, simply sat there. Luckily, there was a nurse enjoying lunch who picked his head up out of his soup. 911 was called and he was hospitalized. It turned out he had changed his medication, and once adjusted, was fine.

On another occasion, a tour from a nursing home brought a bus-load of elderly residents for lunch. They had no idea where they were going, as it was meant to be a mystery tour. Unfortunately, instead of eliciting excitement, the deep woods heightened their anxiety. When they arrived, they wouldn't get off the bus. They were too afraid, out in the middle of the woods with no sidewalks! As fate would have it, Dave Maynard of WBZ (an AM radio station in Boston) happened to be visiting for lunch. Thinking they would listen to a local radio personality, David asked Mr. Maynard if he could help. Mr. Maynard boarded the bus and thankfully convinced them to come in. To Judith's dismay, they refused to eat any food with herbs, opting only for peanut butter and jelly sandwiches!

Then there were those who took offense to some Pickity doings, such as employing a fortune teller for a small weekend festival. Many presumed that by association, Pickity was invoking some kind of malevolent energy. One of the gardens, called The Witches Garden, also presented a problem for some, as it was designed to grow both 'good' and 'bad' plants. A Mugwort cross, hung outside the kitchen door on St. John's Eve to symbolize blessing and protection, would cause a yearly uproar. Judith received many accusatory letters filled with people's wild assumptions. Judith and David engaged in a simple life with time-honored customs. Their intentions were always pure and meant for the good of all.

A memorable "huge mistake" was not advertising one year. The decision to spend their annual investment of fifty thousand dollars somewhere else took its toll as customers thought they had closed! While the best advertising was always 'word of mouth', they learned the hard way to supplement with radio and newspaper advertising.

Cheddar Chive Chips

Photo by Brian Woodbury

½ lb. (2 cups) shredded cheddar cheese
2 TBS finely chopped fresh Chives
1 ½ cup flour
dash of cayenne
½ cup soft butter
½ tsp salt

Combine the cheese, butter, salt, cayenne, and Chives. Add the flour. Divide the dough in half and shape each into a log about 1 ½" in diameter. Wrap in wax paper and chill. Slice into 1/8" slices and bake on a lightly greased sheet at 350 for 10 minutes or until lightly browned. Makes about 4 dozen.

(left) One of the original Pickity catalogues; an older full color catalogue; Judith meets Tasha Tudor

In Pickity's second year, a mail order catalogue was created. It became so popular David quit his job as purchasing manager to help the business full time. David inherently trusted the universe and always "knew" everything would be okay, so leaving came easily. Particular "Pickity" products were chosen for the catalogue and Pat Spaulding of Athol, Massachusetts was hired to do the artwork, "Pickity" style. Each edition was a work of art, created by hand, long before computers or digital photography! Mail order storage took over the porch off the small dining room, and a mailing list was compiled from existing customers. Eventually, other mailing lists and a tracking service were purchased. Part of the barn was revamped for storage and an employee was hired as product 'picker' and shipper. One year, the catalogue was printed by an outsourced service and mailed to one hundred thousand customers with the wrong phone number on it! At the end of seven years, the size and scope of the catalogue became too large to handle with so small a staff, and it was discontinued.

As any entrepreneur knows, you do what you have to do to survive. You store 'the great ideas' until the time is ripe and do the job that will feed your kids. Finances were supplemented in the early years by driving a plow truck for the town of Mason. David also had a Jeep Wrangler for maintaining the long driveway and towing customers out of snowbanks. There were many who would hit their brakes too hard descending Nutting Hill and slide into a particular tree which is visibly scarred today. The Walter's dog would run for hours alongside those plowing trips, trying to keep up. David would always offer a ride but was usually refused, as Duncan preferred to chase.

The frost heaves on wintery roads would thaw into mud in the spring and tires could sink in deep. In an attempt to smooth out the ruts, David would pull a bed spring behind their tractor. It used to be quite a precarious trip to visit Pickity! Understandably, most customers were not willing to drive on the snowy or mucky roads. The Walter's experimented with closing the business Christmas through April for a couple of years, only to have to find and rehire a dependable crew each season - not an easy accomplishment in the middle of nowhere!! From then on, they chose to stay open year-round, despite some harsh winters.

Overcoming the challenges they faced and the importance of staying true to a lifestyle, Pickity grew. Once established and open regular hours, it took about thirty employees to run. Managing that many people calls for clear communication and standard operating procedures, which comes with experience and practice. David took on the role to the best of his abilities. He could pretty much bank on daily issues like someone calling in sick and would usually do their job in addition to his. His acceptance of remiss employees was to simply "keep on keepin' on". He enjoyed the life they had created and wouldn't often let employees disappoint him.

Dear Wendy Walter,

.Thankyou very much for your unique letter. I think it is so good of you to be so thoughtful of your mother in wishing to do something for her that would give her pleasure. I feel honoured that she likes my books, and touched too by your feelings for her. You must be an extra special daughter indeed.

Unfortunately, I simply cannot get away from home, as I have animals and a great deal of art work. This last must be finished by a certain date so I cannot take time away.

Also, I dislike calling people up, maybe you could call me instead? 802-254-9128. The evening is the best time to call, as then I — sure to be on hand and near the telephone. I milk my goats at 9:30 so call before than, that is, if you do call.

I enjoyed your poem. Maybe someday you will be publishing books too!

With best wishes,

Tasha Tudor

To Wendy Walter
October 1, 1979

Along with management, David's duties included directing people to park properly (an antidote to Judith's refusal for white lines painted in the driveway), socializing with customers, and storytelling! Occasionally, a school bus load of children would come for a tour. David would start the tour at the end of the 'short path', and the kids were greeted by Duncan. He would read *Little Red Riding Hood* and then lead them all on a hike down the path with dog simulating the Big Bad Wolf. Their adventure would end in the restaurant for a 'grandmother's basket' lunch. Once they returned to school, the children would often send 'thank you' drawings.

Over the years, the Pickity children were also employed. Shelly, Wendy, Michael, and Andrew were to weed gardens, 'bag herbs' to be sold in the shop, and later work in the restaurant. They spent many hours on the porch off the dining room, bagging, weighing, and labeling dried herbs. Luckily, an in-ground pool, installed in 1978, was accessible off the back porch. Long summer days were spent working, stopping for a dip in the pool for a round of 'Marco Polo' with neighbors, and then back to work. One of their very first jobs was to turn small fabric pockets inside right. The pockets would come sewn up on three sides and would eventually get filled with spice for 'spice strings'. They were paid one cent per bag and learned that speed could be quite lucrative!

When they weren't 'working' or in school, they were making things to sell in the shop, building forts in the woods, hanging out in their tree house, playing in the hay loft, or engaging the neighbors in games like 'Kick the can', 'Ghost', or 'Seven steps around the house'. Not allowed to watch television, except cartoons on Saturday mornings, they were generally outside, unaware of the challenges their parents faced, but intuitive enough to know what would help or hinder.

In 1979, in an attempt to please her mother, Wendy wrote a letter to Tasha Tudor informing her of Judith's admiration and would she please call her as a birthday gift? Ms. Tudor did reply with a letter which was displayed in "Grandmother's Room" for many years. Much later, Judith spoke with Tasha Tudor by phone and met her at a speaking engagement. She also met Tudor's daughter Efner, who enjoyed a Pickity lunch on occasion.

How one responds to challenges reveals character. If a hurricane or a tornado blows through, the determined will endlessly rebuild. Others might give up and leave. The maintenance alone on a house built in the1700's was evidence enough of David and Judith's commitment. Tending to their garden of dreams strengthened their resolve. Each sprinkle of water, each layer of compost, each day of weeding, each bit of faith, accumulated enough intention to overcome growing pains and obstacles.

July

The month of July celebrates summer's abundance of fruits, vegetables, and herbs. Celebrated in England is Swithin's Day, July 15. Rain on St. Swithin's Day means 40 days of drought. Apples watered by a St. Swithin's Day rain become the most delicious.

July, the seventh month in our calendar, was originally the fifth month of the year. The name Julius (July) was given in honor of Julius Caesar, who was born in this month. Anglo-Saxons called July, "Mead Month" because the Meadows were in full-bloom.

Medieval scientists took sun and star measurements on St. Swithin's Day to design almanacs for the coming year. These guides helped determine the proper time for planting, harvesting, and traveling.

It is July, and we are on our knees daily to keep ahead of the weeds! We are happy to have great bunches of fresh flowers for the dining room: Golden Marguerite and yellow Day Lilies, deep blue Hyssop, and the brilliant red Bee Balm.

The harvesting of many wildflowers for drying has begun; as many as 300 bunches a day must be bundled with an elastic and hung from the rafters in the barn. Already, we are picking purple Lustrife, white Yarrow, and Hops Clover. Soon, St. John's Wort will be added to the list. The Mint is ready for its first haircut; we find it benefits from frequent cutting and sometimes harvest it three times during the summer.

We watched the roadsides for Pearly Everlasting and pick it early, just as the blossoms are forming. Fields of yellow Goldenrod beckon to us!

For a tasty summertime snack, we stuff long stalks of the Egyptian onion with cream cheese and stir tall glasses of cold spiced tea with long cinnamon sticks.

July offers us a fine variety of fragrant blossoms for making little bouquets called "tussie mussies". Each flower has a special meaning and conveys a message to the recipient! We select Rosemary for remembrance, Sage for immortality, Thyme for bravery, Borage for courage, and Lavender for good wishes.

The bees are busy in the Thyme, and the hummingbirds are stealing sweet nectar from the Trumpet Vine. We enjoy a late evening walk, armed with Pennyroyal to ward off the mosquitoes! Gallon jugs stand in stately rows filled with a variety of herb vinegars. Opal Basil, Tarragon, Mint, and a blend of seven herbs are our favorites.

The garden offers a myriad of flowers for enhancing succulent dishes from the kitchen: Nasturtiums, Heart's Ease, Borage flowers, and Calendula petals greet surprised luncheon guests!

July is a busy time, for we are eager to garner all the benefits we can from Mother Earth.

Walter, Judy (1984) *The Pickity Place Cookbook*, Mason, NH
Herb Farm Press

August

August is called "high summer" or "hohsum" and celebrates the fulfillment of the growing season. This is the time of Lammastide, when the first loaves of bread baked from the new crop of wheat were consecrated. Gates of the harvest fields were opened and sheep and other animals were allowed to graze on these "Lammas Fields". Every townhouse, country cottage, and noble castle shared a lammas feast.

The spirit of the wheat was preserved in the corn dolly, made from the last sheaf of corn. The ancient craft of corn dolly making goes back thousands of years when it was thought that a spirit lived in the cornfield which died when the corn (wheat) was cut. To preserve this spirit and insure the success of next year's harvest, a corn idol was made for this spirit to rest in. The corn dolly has become a decorative symbol of peace and prosperity in the home throughout the year.

The hot, lazy days of August, often called "dog days", wear us to a frazzle. Our Irish Setter, Duncan, has dug a hole in the damp ground under the lilac tree, hoping for a cool spot in which to rest. We pray for a cooling shower or even a thunderstorm to clear the air, and have faith that our Mugwort cross on the roof will protect us from lightning! An icy glass of lemon balm tea is a welcome respite.

The Goldenrod is ripening, and we wade into the swamps to collect great bunches of Joe Pye weed. We have decorated the dining room with a collection of corn dollies and bunches of wheat to celebrate the Lammastide. Fruit is a ripening on the pear tree, and we checked to see if the elderberries are ready for jelly making. If so, we will have purple fingers for a day or two! A mourning dove has taken up residence nearby and we hear his mournful sigh in the early evening hours.

The growing season has begun to wind down, and the days are getting shorter. Hopefully, it has been a fruitful season, and we relax a bit and are happy with the fruits of our labors.

Walter, Judy (1984) *The Pickity Place Cookbook*, Mason, NH Herb Farm Press

September

Traditionally, Michaelmas day was celebrated on September 29 and honored the archangel St. Michael. The festival signified the end of the harvest time in medieval Europe. It is one of the four quarters of the year when rent and bills came due, and often a goose was included in the payment of rent to the landlord!

In England, a large glove was suspended from a pole on the town hall to signal that the Michaelmas fair was to begin. Merchants and craftsmen came from miles around to sell their wares.

A Michaelmas feast must include a roasted goose, for it was believed that, "if you eat a goose on St. Michaelmas day you will never want for money all the year round"!

Ginger was traditionally served in at least one of the feast dishes. Saint Michael was believed to be a healer and Guardian, and medieval physicians considered Ginger to be a healing herb and important for protection against infection.

The New England Aster blooms at the time of the Michaelmas feast and is known as the Michaelmas Daisy.

September, and the scent of ripening grapes is in the air. The first tart apples are ready and we bring a bushel into the shop for customers to munch on as they browse.

Back into the greenhouse come the tender herbs and Scented Geraniums, overflowing their pots with their summer growth, and ready to give us winter cuttings. The greenhouse is restocked with plants for winter windowsills –Chives, Rosemary, Tarragon, Thyme, Scented Geraniums, and Sweet Bay.

The Silver King Artemisia is ripe for picking now that the tiny seed heads have formed, and large bunches hang from the rafters. The top of the barn is filled with summer's bounty, and the colors of the drying flowers and herbs is glorious – deep purple and yellow Statice, white Everlasting and Yarrow, magenta Oregano blossoms, pink Chives, and orange-yellow Goldenrod.

Teasel stands in tall baskets with Dock and other brown grasses from the fields, and smaller baskets hold Rosehips and seed pods.

It is now that we begin making our herbal wreaths, stuffing the wreath wires with Silver King and Mugwort, then decorating them with colorful dried flowers, seed pods, and spices – Cinnamon sticks, whole Nutmeg, and Ginger root.

Tiny bird nests are filled with dried bouquets, and our imaginations run wild with this new bounty of materials to work with!

Already we are thinking ahead and planning for the holidays soon to come.

Walter, Judy (1984) *The Pickity Place Cookbook*, Mason, NH Herb Farm Press

The Harvest

Nature herself does not distinguish between what seed it receives. It grows whatever seed is planted; this is the way life works. Be mindful of the seeds you plant today, as they will become the crop you harvest."

Mary Morrissey

The Harvest marks the end of the growing season, and is the most labor-intensive time of year. Its social importance makes it the focus of seasonal celebrations such as Lammas, meaning 'loaf mass', originally celebrated on August 1st. Farmers baked bread from the new wheat crop and provided it to their local church as the Communion bread for a special Mass to thank God for the harvest.

Celebrating the harvest each fall at Pickity Place started with bushels of apples, set out as a free snack for customers. Hundreds of bunches of herbs such as Mugwort, Silver King, and Artemisia were cut and hung to dry from the rafters of the barn for future wreaths. The whole family participated in the harvest of Loosestrife, Joe Pye Weed, Goldenrod, Yarrow, and Tansy, usually amassed along roadsides somewhere. Judith turned the loot into about 50 wreaths a year and sold hundreds of bunches of dried flowers for others to make their own. Pumpkins were the most obvious sign that harvest time had come, and summer had succumbed to autumn.

By 1981, "Pickity" had completely taken over the house and property. Even the bedrooms were needed for offices. The family packed up and moved back to New Ipswich, where David and Judith commuted for the next twenty years. Eventually, Pickity provided enough income for the Walter's to hire a full-time manager, affording them a part-time commitment. It wasn't until 1999 though, when David felt he had reached his financial goal of grossing $1,000,000 in a single year.

Judith had shaped her passions into a form through which others could see, touch, smell, taste, and come to know her world. She transformed gardens from alive to teeming with bees and butterflies, and shared the fruits of her efforts through her cooking. Some of her sincerest devotees shared comments such as:

"You have Shangri-La here. You've got it all over Martha Stewart. Food was outrageous, service wonderful."

"Every time we come here we feel enervated, yet relaxed, inspired and peaceful. We like to take that feeling home with us."

"This luncheon surpasses anything Martha Stewart presents - really!"

You could find Judith's aspiration toward perfection in everything she touched. In fact, there is a family joke about her perfect and speedy bow tying ability! A skill which none of her children practiced enough to emulate. Bows were tied on many, if not most, of the products in the shop as a finishing touch.

(left) Andrew carving a pumpkin on the brick patio outside the greenhouse 1977; Thanksgiving in what is now the small dining room circa 1978; Wendy and Michael carving pumpkins on the brick patio outside the greenhouse 1977; Scarecrow outside the front door early 1990's..

Chicken Crepes with Herbs and Cider

2 large boned chicken breasts cut into strips
2 TBS Butter
1/2 tsp herb salt substitute
1 onion, minced
2 tsp Parsley, chopped
1/4 tsp Thyme
1/4 tsp Rosemary
2/3 cup apple cider
1 cup half and half
2 TBS cornstarch
12 warm cooked crepes

Saute the chicken in the butter for 3 minutes. Stir in the onions, spices and cider. Cover and simmer about 10 minutes until chicken is tender. Remove chicken from the cider mixture; keep chicken warm. Combine half and half with cornstarch. Add to the cider mixture and cook on low heat, stirring until thickened. Place about 2 TBS chicken and 1 TBS sauce on each crepe. Roll up and cover with additional sauce. Serve immediately.

Photo by Brian Woodbury

Photo by Brian Woodbury

Pumpkin Parfait

1 package Vanilla pudding mix
1/4 cup light brown sugar
1/2 teaspoon Cinnamon
1/4 teaspoon Ginger
1 1/2 cups milk
1 cup prepared pumpkin

Combine the dry ingredients. Heat the milk to boiling and add the pumpkin and dry ingredients. Mix well. Spoon into serving glasses and top with whipped cream and chopped nuts.

59

Some of the signposts along the way to a successful Pickity harvest were radio and TV appearances. Liz Walker, a television news anchor for WBZ-TV, visited in 1982. Later, a camera crew for 'Chronicle', a newsmagazine television series which premiered on WCVB on January 25, 1982, showed up to include Pickity in an episode. Local, Boston, and other newspapers and magazines featured Pickity over sixty times.

The ever-growing clientele, impressed with the unique character and delicious food of the tea house, persisted in demanding recipes. Judith responded with *The Pickity Place Cookbook* in 1984, highlighting the monthly festivals, and *A Walk Through Our Kitchen Garden* in 1985, a compilation of what she taught on her garden tours.

In *The Pickity Place Cookbook, Unlocking the Magic of Herbs*, Volume III, published in 1993, Judith wrote:

"It is hard for us to believe that it has been 16 years since the inception of Pickity Place. For those of you who have just discovered us we started with just a small shop in the carriage shed adjacent to our 200 -year- old house. Over these 16 years, we have grown to include a nationwide mail order catalogue, a large gift shop, bookshop and museum room, greenhouse and what this book is all about – the Pickity Place Restaurant. Many of you will remember the 'Pickity Kids', our children who helped out from age 5 and up; they gardened and worked as dishwashers, waitresses and maintenance 'men' and always as taste testers for the restaurant menus. Three of those children are now college graduates with one to go!"

A fourth volume, *Country Herb Cooking*, was commissioned by Smithmark Publishers of NY. As pleased as Judith was to have a publisher pursue her, she was disappointed with their choice of artwork for the jacket cover. She pleaded with them to go with something more 'Pickity', but to no avail. They published the book with an orange cover and a kitchen scene. A second edition was later self-published by the family with her cover of preference. Her version sold out!

In 1993, David Berry, a chef at Disney World, was asked to create a gingerbread house with a storyland theme. He thought of his visits to Pickity Place and made an exact replica. When the display was dismantled, he drove it to New Hampshire in the back of his pickup truck to present it to David and Judy. His ingredients included 25 pounds of gingerbread, 600 pieces of Big Red gum, 360 pieces of Dentyne gum, four pounds of crushed black pepper, 51 pounds of royal icing, and two pounds of salt dough.

Pickity turned twenty in 1996, and the anniversary was celebrated as a year-long "harvest festival" in appreciation of its loyal customers. All that year's events were infused with enthusiasm for their accomplishment. They hosted a "show us your picture of Pickity" photography contest, a twentieth anniversary T-shirt design contest, had a visit from the Easter Bunny during the annual kids Easter egg hunt, a visit from Santa at Christmastime, and new classes on how to craft.

After twenty-five years of non-stop work, David and Judith felt the need for change. They defined their success through the satisfaction of knowing people came to their place out in the middle of nowhere and liked it! Inspiring others and hearing about the impact of Pickity spelled success for them very early on. Of course, growing a financially viable business was crucial for their retirement, but money was never the principal motivator. Their harvest was evidenced by a well-loved farm life, reasonably early retirement, and now four grandchildren. As Pickity Place took on a life of its own, David and Judith knew it was time to start a new adventure.

(above) Camera crew with Liz Walker and Judith 1982, David and Judith at Crotched Mountain ski slope for a WBZ promotion. Bottom: Liz Walker and Judith 1982; TV camera crew.

— Volume III —

THE
Pickity Place™

COOKBOOK

Unlocking the magic of herbs . . .

The Pickity PLACE™ Cookbook

Pickity PLACE®

A Walk Through Our Kitchen Garden

By Judy Walter

• Herbs
• Legends
• Recipes

COUNTRY HERB COOKING

Four Seasons of Recipes from Pickity Place

JUDY WALTER

Dear Oma,

Magic runs deep within you,
And I am so grateful to share your lineage
Of the Earth whisperers,
The secret of which flows deep in our veins.
You have shown me what it is like to love something
Into beauty, with each flower that blooms by your touch
I can feel the love that blossoms between you and that flower.
I envy you grandmother!
What a gift! What power! What Love!

I remember asking you how you plan your garden
And the answer was always
"I just feel and know where things are supposed to go,
it's like the plants
Are speaking to me. So I listen and it works out."

What wisdom you must have, something so deep that words
Cannot speak of the ways in which it manifests.
The wisdom, the magic the power, the beauty
That is what I see you as.
Never can the confusion of life alter my perception of
Who and what you are.

Love, your Grandson,
Zachary

Letter/Poem to Judith from Grandson Zachary Adinolfi; Right: Two prints by
Mary Azarian used frequently to decorate the dining rooms.

Spicy Pomanders

Select firm, medium- sized apples or oranges. You may also use crab apples, kumquats, limes, or lemons. You will need good quality cloves that are longed stemmed and unbroken. Insert one clove at a time to cover fruit entirely. Complete within 24 hours. For the rolling mix combine:

8 oz. ground cinnamon
4 oz. ground cloves
1 oz. ground ginger
4 oz. of ground orris root

Place the spice mixture in a large, open bowl. Add the clove-covered fruit and turn until well coated. Leave the fruit in this mixture, turning once each day. To hang, thread a large- eyed needle with narrow ribbon and run it through the fruit. Tie with a bow and add a loop at the top for hanging.

Photo by Brian Woodbury

Photo by Brian Woodbury

Pumpkin Nut Roll

3 eggs
1 cup sugar
2/3 cup pumpkin
1 tsp lemon juice
¾ cup flour
½ tsp ginger
1 tsp baking powder
2 tsp cinnamon
½ tsp nutmeg
1 cup chopped nuts

Beat the eggs 5 minutes at high speed. Gradually beat in the sugar. Stir in the pumpkin and lemon juice. Stir together the dry ingredients and fold them into the pumpkin mixture. Line a jellyroll pan with waxed paper and spread on the mixture. Top with the walnuts. Bake at 375º for 15 minutes. Turn the cake out onto a linen towel, dusted with confectioner's sugar. Start at narrow end and roll towel and cake together. Cool thoroughly. Unroll, spread with filling, roll up, and chill.

Lemon Olive Meatballs

1 lb. Hamburger
3 TBS lemon juice
1 tsp, Herb salt
4oz sharp cheddar, grated
12 small green olives, finely chopped
¼ Green Pepper, finely chopped
1 Cup herb seasoned bread crumbs
1 Egg
¼ Cup milk
12-15 slices bacon, partially cooked

Mix together the beef, lemon juice, and herb salt. Add the grated cheese, olives, pepper, bread crumbs, milk, and egg. Shape into small balls and wrap each with 1/3rd slice of the partially cooked bacon and secure with a toothpick. Bake at 375º for 20-25 minutes. Serve hot.

Photos by Brian Woodbury

Curried Coriander Soup

2 TBS butter
1 tsp ground coriander
½ tsp ground cumin
2 TBS flour
3 ¾ cup chicken broth, heated
juice of ½ lemon
dash black pepper
2/3 cup light cream
1/3 cup cooked rice

Heat the butter in a saucepan and stir in the ground coriander and cumin. Stir over low heat 1 minute, then add the flour. Stir for 2 minutes, then add the heated stock. Stir until blended and simmer for 4 minutes. Add the lemon juice and pepper. Stir in the cream and the cooked rice and heat. Serve with croutons.

October

Halloween is the end of the year in the ancient pagan Celtic calendar, and was called Summer's End, or "Samhain".

October brings to mind piles of glowing pumpkins, baskets overflowing with nuts and fruits, and a warming cup of hot mulled cider.

Halloween is the holiday signaling the entrance into winter, and October is the time when ghosts, spirits, and witches were thought to be most powerful and most lonely. Early witches wore capes of purple to suggest the darkness, which they loved, or dark blue to represent the night, in which they worked their spells.

A witch's broom was always made of ash and bound with willow twigs. In ancient Greece, Celery seeds were thought to keep witches from falling off their brooms!

The first frost has come, and each night we must cover the orange mound of pumpkins piled in the old wagon. On sunny days, the hillsides are ablaze in their autumn finery, and a brisk walk along the path in the woods is exhilarating!

The old wood burning cook stove is keeping us warm and cozy in the shop, and a pot of hot mulled cider bubbling on top greets guests coming in from the cold. Old friends are coming by for their stock of winter herbs and spices and perhaps a dried bouquet to liven up the winter months ahead.

Out come the brown-checked tablecloths in the dining room, and the mantle is decorated with Bittersweet, apples, nuts, pumpkins, and gourds. Braided Indian corn decorates one wall and an herbal wreath in brown and gold tones another.

Halloween is one of our favorite holidays, and crossed sticks in the form of "witch's crofts" are hung in the windows. Cornhusks, dried and then dyed black, are crafted into witches, with corn silk for hair. The old black velvet cape hangs on a peg by the door, beside the broom with the twisted handle.

The witch's garden has been trimmed back, and an ancient cauldron hangs from its tripod against the stone wall.

We have started making pomander balls, filling apples and oranges with whole Cloves. These are rolled in a spicy mixture and put by the wood stove to dry. A cricket has come in from the cold, and we let him stay for good luck!

The gardens are looking stark now, but we still enjoy the texture of the gray Santolina and the Southernwood as it waves gracefully. It is time to think about mulching the Lavenders and putting them to bed for the winter.

Walter, Judy (1984) *The Pickity Place Cookbook,* Mason, NH Herb Farm Press

November

Martinmas, traditionally celebrated on November 11th, is a feast day of St. Martin, a patron saint of the French. Martinmas falls at the end of the harvest season and is celebrated with feasts and new wine. In ancient Europe, the children received apples and nuts. Harvesters paraded through the streets carrying lanterns and singing.

St. Catherine day is also celebrated in November. The wheel is the symbol of her death in the 14th century. Flaming wheels of fire were whirled by a juggler. These were called "Catherine Wheels". Above the feast table was hung a chandelier, above a frothy pot of hot mulled cider and apples. This was the "Cathern" bowl.

As you prepare for the holidays, put some Mugwort in your shoes to keep your feet rested. It is known as the "herb for the weary traveler".

Leaves rustle under the eaves, the days are short, and the first damp smell of snow is in the air. Helpers come in with loads of wood and their noses are red!

We are busy, busy, busy, making herbal goodies for the holidays. The shop is filling up with gifts: mortars filled with herbs and tied with a calico bow, Mugwort pillows for dreaming on, bags of wood stove incense and herbal soaps in baskets tied up with pretty ribbons. Hand-dipped candles scented with Bayberry or Cranberry hang from an old wagon wheel. We're aging 25 pounds of Christmas pine potpourri for holiday shoppers, and the larger Rosemary plants have been trimmed to sell as miniature Christmas trees.

Our shelves are stocked with spices and herbs for holiday baking: Cardamom for sweet breads, Anise for Springerle cookies, and Vanilla beans for making your own Kahlúa. We bring out the candied Angelica and real Licorice sticks.

Now that the winter winds are whistling in the chimney, we take pleasure in seeing the wood, all split and stacked in the barn.

This is the time of year when we are most busy with our mail-order catalog, and stacks of boxes are lined up by the kitchen door, waiting for their journey to eager recipients. We must take time out from this rush to be thankful we are busy!

Walter, Judy (1984) *The Pickity Place Cookbook,* Mason, NH
Herb Farm Press

December

St. Lucia's day is December 13, which celebrates the festival of light, the winter solstice. St. Lucia was especially venerated by those people living where winter nights are very long and dark.

In Swedish homes today, the youngest daughter is chosen to be the Lucia Queen. She rises early, and wearing a white gown and a crown of lighted candles, brings breakfast and a song to members of her household and to the animals on the farm. We were surprised indeed when our daughter, Wendy, woke us early on this day to carry out the tradition!

St. Nicholas is the patron saint of sailors, travelers, baker's, merchants, and especially children. An old legend tells of his giving gold to each of three girls who had no dowries, and thus were unable to marry. St. Nicholas day is December 6 and much of Europe still celebrates this special day.

The Dutch brought the "Visit of St. Nicholas" to America; the name "Santa Clause" comes from Sinter Klass, Dutch for St. Nicholas.

Bring the fresh scents of evergreens in for the holiday decorating! Mistletoe, the plant of peace, banishes evil spirits and protects homes against thunder and lightning. Holly protects against witches and the evil eye. Rosemary signifies remembrance and friendship. Laurel protects and purifies, and is symbolic of victory, distinction, and honor.

Christmas festivities signal the culmination of our labors throughout the year. Decorating for this beloved holiday is a joyful task! A fragrant tree is cut and stands in one corner of the dining room. It is brought in on the first day of December so it can be enjoyed by our luncheon guests throughout the month. Our tree decorations are handmade: cornhusk angels, hand carved doves, Cinnamon sticks tied with bright red ribbons, strings of red wooden beads, and chains made from wood chips.

Fresh evergreens and Laurel from the woods nearby are placed about with abandon - on the mantle and windowsills and tucked into cupboards. Red candles in tin candle holders brighten tables and a Swedish straw stag stands under the tree.

A wooden shoe is placed on the mantle to honor St. Nicholas. In this, we place a branch of Broom Plant to represent black peters switches, Teasel to represent the cloth merchants, and yellow Tansy to represent the bags of gold St. Nicholas gave to charity.

Close your eyes and imagine the pungent odors of orange and spice of the Pomander, the sweet scents of Roses and Lavender and other ingredients of the winter potpourri, the wood smoke from the fireplace, and the wonderful spicy aromas from the kitchen!

Christmas - a time for family and friends, inspiration, and a look back over the blessings of the year.

Walter, Judy (1984) *The Pickity Place Cookbook*, Mason, NH Herb Farm Press

The Festivals & Gardens

The Margaret and Carl Walter Family Christmas Tree circa 1940's;
The raised garden beds behind the gift shop circa 1985.

Part of the magic of *Being Pickity* was there was always something to celebrate! Colorful decorations, crafting, and traditions instilled a sense of wonder and anticipation. The festivals, combined with herbal lore, provided the elements from which to conjure up unique recipes, crafts, and concoctions.

Each month signaled new festivities. The family's traditions were guided by convention, but emphasized celebrating the Earth, not religion. Most importantly, the festivals provided fun and a sense of hope. New Year's Eve came with plenty of newspaper confetti, a tradition their son Mike started. His ritual would begin shortly after Christmas, filling several grocery bags with cut up newspaper. The stroke of midnight would bring a magnificent paper storm. Valentine's Day encompassed a couple of weeks rather than a single day. A homemade box put out in advance was filled with handmade cards and notes. A special dinner was convened on Valentine's Day and all the notes would be read to each other. Easter came with an annual family egg hunt, and May Day with a dance around the maypole. To this day, Judith makes a May basket and sneaks over to Brookline, New Hampshire to put on Wendy's doorstep. Halloween included handmade costumes and trick or treating by car, as houses were too far apart.

While Christmas was the most conspicuous celebration of the year, December festivities also included St. Lucia's Day on the 13th.

"In Swedish homes today, the youngest daughter is chosen to be Lucia Queen. She rises early, and wearing a white gown and crown of lighted candles, brings breakfast and a song to members of her household and the animals on the farm. We were surprised indeed when our daughter Wendy, woke up early on this day to carry out the tradition!" (Walter p.221)

Wendy decided at age eleven, as the youngest girl in the house, to deliver St. Lucia buns. That year she snuck around gathering candles for a wreath that was worn on her head. She woke up early on December 13th, stole buns from the kitchen, crammed the lit wreath onto her head, and tiptoed into her parent's bedroom in her nightgown. The candle light was striking in the dark of the early morning and Judith and David were truly stunned to wake to their daughter with fire on her head.

To kick off each Christmas season, the children searched the woods for a small tree to put up in their bedrooms. There was no requirement to do so. It was just an idea, "You want to put a tree up in your room? What a great idea; what a fantastic way to keep kids busy decorating their own tree!" They strung popcorn and cranberries and painted wooden ornaments. They made paper globes from Christmas cards, garlands, and wreaths. They also made a lot of their gifts, but would go on one shopping excursion each December to the mall in Manchester with the money they earned, plus a little extra from their parents. At the mall, the six of them would split up; a shopping night for the kids. It was a thrill and a testament to how times have changed!

The family tree was set up on Christmas Eve in the living room. Positioning the Christmas tree was a production, with a bucket full of stones for stabilizing the trunk and a wire strung from the top of the tree to the wall. Santa decorated and transformed the entire room. The tree sparkled, the stockings were full, and a pickle ornament hid, waiting to be found. Grandma Walter's Christmas Bread would be ready to slather with butter, and a letter from Santa awaited the eager children.

Mike's confetti circa 1981; Wendy dressed as St. Lucia 1979; The dining room Christmas tree with straw ornaments.

Grandma Berry's Plum Pudding

½ C Butter
½ C Molasses
1 C. Figs
1 C. Dates
3 ½ C Flour
½ tsp Cloves
½ tsp Nutmeg
1 tsp Baking Soda
⅓ C Brown Sugar
1 C Milk
1 tsp Cinnamon

Combine the butter and brown sugar, add the molasses. Add the milk and dry ingredients alternately. Steam for 2 ½ hours in a steam pudding mold (my grandmother would use a tin can).

For the hard sauce, mix ½ C butter, 1 cup confectioners' sugar, ¼ C brandy (or cream), and add extra sugar as needed.

When served, pour hot rum or brandy over the pudding and ignite. Don't burn your hair!

Christmas pudding has its origins in medieval England, and is sometimes known as plum pudding, Christmas Pudding, or just "pud". Despite the name "plum pudding," it contains no actual plums. Pre-Victorian use of the word "plums" meant raisins.

Grandma Walter's Christmas Bread

6 cups Flour
3 cups Milk
½ lb Butter, melted
1 cup Sugar
½ tsp Lemon Rind
1 pkg Yeast dissolved in 2 TBS warm water
½ lb Currents
¼ lb blanched Almonds
¼ lb diced Citron
¼ tsp Salt
1 ½ TBS Lemon juice
½ lb raisins
¼ tsp Mace

In a large bowl, make a well in the 6 cups of flour and add all the remaining ingredients in order. Work all into the flour and mix well. Cover with a damp towel and let rise for 12 hours. Beat well. Pour into 2 greased 41/2" x 9 ½" loaf pans. Let rise until double. Bake at 350° 1 hour. Remove from pans and while hot, spread tops with melted butter and a heavy coating of confectioner's sugar. Sprinkle lightly with rose water.

Christmas morning started with stockings and then the presents were opened in turn, one by one. It occupied most of the day! Shrimp cocktail kept appetites satiated until Christmas "dinner" was served around one o'clock.

Dessert included Grandma Berry's (Judith's mother) Plum Pudding, a dense brown bread served with a hard sweet sauce. It was always brought to the table doused with brandy or rum and then lit on fire.

With age, the children questioned the reality of Santa. The year Wendy asked her parents for a direct answer, she didn't get the one she wanted. "No, Santa's not real". Well, Wendy got motivated to prove them wrong! She stayed up late Christmas Eve that year and, while her parents thought she was sound asleep, she dressed up in red, found some cotton to make a beard, and a red sack. She snuck into each of her sibling's rooms and took the presents from under their trees, a job traditionally for 'Santa', and stuffed the sack. She headed down the back stairs toward the living room very quietly and went right to the cookies, took a bite, read the letters as if she was Santa, and started stuffing the stockings with gifts. She sincerely thought she was disguised enough to be unrecognizable and thankfully her parents played along, not saying a word as they watched from the couch with humor.

The Festivals

January 6th ~ Epiphany (or Three Kings Day), a feast day celebrating the revelation of God incarnate as Jesus Christ, and Janus on the 9th, celebrating the god of transitions as we move into a new year.

February 14th ~ St. Valentine's Day and Shrove Tuesday, the day before Ash Wednesday.

March 20 or 21~ Vernal Equinox

April ~ Carling Sunday, the fifth Sunday in Lent, when Carling peas are served, and Easter.

May 1st ~ May Day Festival

June ~ Summer solstice (varies between the 20th and 22nd), St. John's Eve on the 23rd and Midsummer festival on the 24th, by Christian tradition, the longest day of the year, though not astronomically.

July 15th ~ St. Swithin's Day, when it is traditionally believed if it rains on the day, it will not rain for the next 40.

August 1st ~ Lammas Festival, the first harvest festival of the year to mark the annual wheat harvest.

September 29th ~ Michaelmas Day, or Archangel Day, when a goose is traditionally served.

October 31st ~ Halloween and Samhain on October 31st-November 1st

November 11th ~ St. Martin's Feast or Martinmas, celebrated as the time when seeding of the autumn wheat was done, and St. Catherine's Day on the 25th, commemorating the martyrdom of St. Catherine of Alexandria with the baking of "Cattern Cakes" and the lighting of the Catherine's Wheel.

December ~ St. Nicholas Day on the 6th, a celebration of St. Nicholas when children leave their shoes by the foyer, hoping for St. Nicholas to come and fill them with coins, **St. Lucia Day on the 13th**, the Christian festival of light celebrating St. Lucia, who wore a wreath of light on her head to light her way through the catacombs to feed the Christians hidden there, **Winter Solstice on the 22nd**, the shortest day of the year, and **Christmas on the 25th**.

Wendy pretends to be Santa; Andrew and Mike hang their stocking over the living room fireplace (what is now the large dining room); Pickity Place gingerbread house made by Dave Berry.

The Gardens

THE WITCHES
GARDEN
HEALING HERBS

THE WITCHES GARDEN
MANY OF THE HERBS
IN THIS GARDEN ARE
POISON

I keep a goat to see him prance,
I carry a staff, I talk to my plants,
I stare in the fire and crook my thumb,
And whatever I see in the flames
I become.

The Witches Garden

Belief in magic and witchcraft is as old as humankind. The witches garden was a collection of herbs used in ancient charms and potions to help those who were ill and sick at heart. The gardens were not intended to portray the modern Wiccan practitioner. When the site was selected, a willow, elder, and a beautiful hawthorn tree were already growing there.

The witches garden contained a center cauldron; the bed on the right had herbs, flowers, and barks used in medicine:

On the left side were plants the "black witch" may have used in potions and spells. The garden was enclosed by a fence with a ball and chain gate.

Agrimony	
Alyssum	
Artemisia	Aconite
Borage	Belladonna
Calendula	Elder
Comfrey	Foxglove
Dill	Hawthorne
Elecampane	Hemlock
Horehound	Lilly of the Valley
Juniper	Mayapple
Mugwort	Nettle
Rue	Parsley
St. John's Wort	Pennyroyal
Valerian	Spurge
Willow	Tansy
Wormwood	Toadflax
	Wolfsbane

Culinary Garden

These were the plants our guests were most familiar with. This marked the beginning of the garden tour with the sign "Please handle the herbs". These plants were later used in the cooking and garnishing of restaurant meals and in making teas.

For cooking and garnishing:
Thyme
Sage
Parsley
Sweet Marjoram
Summer and Winter Savories
Cilantro
Tarragon
Chives
Oregano
Basil
Dill
Caraway
Rosemary
Sweet Bay
Sweet Cicely
Angelica
Coriander
Salad Burnet
Lovage
Chervil
Egyptian onion

For Teas:
Hyssop
Bee balm
Mints
Lemon Balm
Comfrey
Lemon Verbena

Edible Flowers:
Viola
Tangerine and lemon Gem Marigolds
Borage
Calendula
Lavender
Nasturtium
Roses

Silver and Grey Garden

This garden required full sun, as most of these plants do not appreciate even slight shade. Many plants do not exhibit showy blooms, but are restful and easy on the eye. Viewing this garden on moonlit nights was especially magical.

Grey Santolina
Lambs Ear
Silver King Artemesia
Silver Mound Artemesia
Clove pink
Dittany of Crete
Curry plant
Horehound
Lavender
Licorice plant
Nepeta
Pearly Everlasting
Clary Sage
Silver Thyme
Garden Sage
Wormwood
Roman Wormwood
Yarrow

Shakespeare Garden

Many of the flowers in English gardens were brought over by the early colonists, along with their lore and uses. Shakespeare's references to these plants inspired the garden,

"I know a bank where the wild thyme grows"
–Midsummer Night's Dream

"Here's flowers for you, hot lavender, sweet mints, savory, marjoram"
– Winter's Tale

"We will plant nettles, sow lettuce, set hyssop and weed up thyme"
– Othello

Lemon Balm
Bay
Burnet
Camonick
Carnation
Flax
Hyssop
Savory
Rosemary
Marjoram
Parsley
Marigold
Pansy
Rue
Thyme
Wormwood
Mint

Dye Garden

Many of the plants included in this garden were colorful annuals and perennials. It was located near the drying shed and was in the shape of a wheel, lined with bricks, with the various plants between the spaces. The four edges outside the circle contained the numerous taller specimens. Plants were the major source for dyes before 1850 and a study of the various colors obtained from them is fascinating!

Anchusa
Ladies Bedstraw
Bloodroot
Scotch Broom
Coltsfoot
Coreopsis
Dyer's Chamomile
Woad
Indigo
Marigold
Parsley
Rue
St. John's Wort
Tansy
Sweet Woodruff
Weld

The Bouquet of Being Pickity

"Any human anywhere will blossom
in a hundred unexpected talents and
capacities simply by being given the
opportunity to do so."

- Doris Lessing

Mishmash of flowers from different gardens
Born and brought up under different stipulation
Cross each other's path suddenly some day
Form a bouquet of great elegance
Each having diverse facets
Yet the flowers do complement each other
Looking at them the spectators feel
These flowers were made to come together

- Kavitha Krishnamurthy

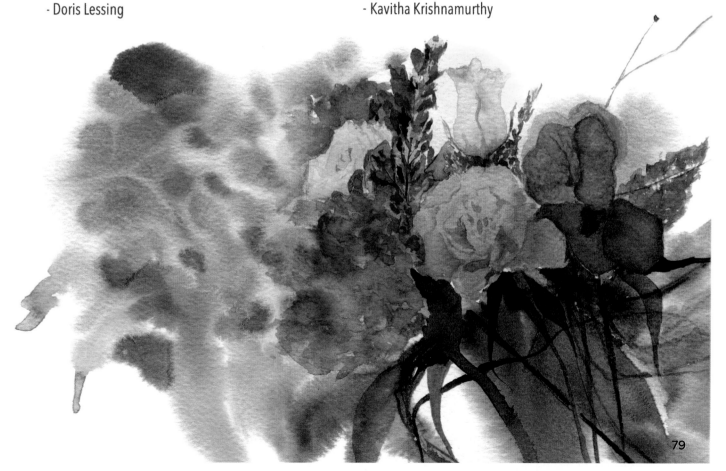

Once blossomed and harvested, plants can be used for a variety of purposes such as food, medicine, and pigment. One of the more popular uses for flowers is the bouquet. Creating a bouquet symbolizes celebration, joy, and the beauty of life. Each sprig or blossom adding its unique quality to the woven symphony of color, texture, and scent. Over the years Judith created many bridal bouquets, choosing each ingredient carefully.

People also blossom as they grow into their power or a better understanding of the "medicine" or nourishment they contribute to the community. As Pickity blossomed into a being unto itself, so did the Walter's.

Pickity Place was sold in 2000 and has since been under the wing of Keith Grimes. It continues its yearly cycle of seedlings, sprouting, growing, blooming, and harvesting. The reverberations of "Being Pickity" has changed many lives and, while David and Judith may have moved on to other things, their energy continues to awaken others to a joyful, earth-centered life; to their power and purpose.

David and Judith spent winters in Key West for a time. They loved Portsmouth, New Hampshire and purchased a condo there. A few years later, they opted for a larger home in Portsmouth where they had plenty of room for children and grandchildren to visit and to keep up traditions for the holidays.

The sale of Pickity Place caused some emotional upheaval – while they were happy to shed a myriad of responsibilities, they were sad to give up part of their original dream. The old home under the Ash tree and a way of life was replaced with the freedom to travel and garden for themselves instead of for an audience.

In 2006, they traveled to Ireland with Wendy and her children, to see their grandson Zachary compete on his harp and a few years later, they had the opportunity to swap homes with a family from the French countryside of Normandy. More recently, they have been spending time in California.

Downsizing from the large house in Portsmouth brought them to Stratham, NH. A small lot for gardening required careful planning. Removing the lawn provided enough space to tend astonishing gardens. In fact, they recently won the Exeter Area Garden Club Award.

(left) David on his bike, Judith at the ocean, David and Judith in their garden 2015; Judith in her garden in Stratham NH 2017; David and Judith in their beloved convertible "Poppy". (right) Shelly on Horse named Rebel 2011; Shelly with Llamas, S'mores and Linda, hiking the John Muir Trail CA 2016; Megan Walter; Sam Walter; The Family from left to right: Megan, Andrew, Valerie, Sam, Judith, David, Wendy, Zachary. (Alexandra is taking the photo and Shelly is in CA).

Alongside gardening, they keep fit with biking and hiking. They spend many hours on the road visiting garden centers and craft fairs. Evenings are spent with a good book and knitting.

Most importantly, they find great satisfaction in looking back at their accomplishments, having helped make their little corner of the earth a better place.

Photo by Lee Peterson

Daughter Shelly followed an intense passion for horses and pursued a degree in Animal Science. Her entrepreneurial upbringing paid off, as she spent years learning and gaining experience in equine breeding, management, and hospital care. She also started a small business boarding horses and teaching riding lessons.

In 2004, she decided to pursue a degree in photography and digital imaging. Graduating at the top of her class offered new opportunities, such as teaching continuing adult education courses and apprenticing with local photographers.

In 2007, she took a full-time job in San Diego, CA working for an architectural firm far from New England's cold winters. To this day she loves the west, working, riding her horse, and taking photographs. She spends all her free time hiking and off-roading in her Jeep along the California Coastal Dunes, high in the alpine of the Sierra Mountains, and through desert canyons.

Son Andrew, always fascinated by how things work, wanted to be in a creative field where things get built. He studied architecture at Roger Williams University in Rhode Island, which offered the only 5- year undergraduate program in the country. Finishing school in the middle of a recession, he and brother Mike started a business maintaining homes on Cape Cod. Eventually, the economy turned and Andrew began to apprentice under an architect and moved to Boston to expand into the field.

Enamored by architecture but not the profession, Andrew began to carve out a niche with technology. Harkening back to his young days at Pickity Place helping dad with spreadsheets on the computer, he saw that there was still opportunity in architecture. He moved up the ranks at a medium-sized national firm that focuses on livable communities. Andrew is now a partner at the firm. In addition to keeping things running, he works with cities and transportation authorities on large-scale mitigation projects. He also works with affordable housing organizations, designing and implementing management systems to allow them to be better at helping others.

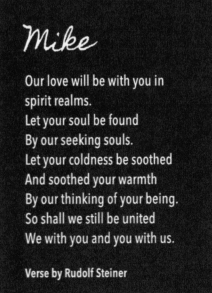

Mike

Our love will be with you in
spirit realms.
Let your soul be found
By our seeking souls.
Let your coldness be soothed
And soothed your warmth
By our thinking of your being.
So shall we still be united
We with you and you with us.

Verse by Rudolf Steiner

Along the way, he married and had two children; Samuel and Megan. Their life is in sharp contrast to growing up Pickity, but they endure stories of the old days, which hopefully someday they will appreciate. Sam appears to be taking on the role of engineer and is a very precise child. Megan likes to get in the dirt. She is the caretaker of many pets, the keeper of the wild gardens, and loves to write. One of their favorite parts of the year is the week at Oma and Opa's house (David and Judith), where they get to experience a little of what it was like to grow up Pickity.

Son Michael, a big hearted, sensitive man who found humor in all things, was quick with a play on words and always had a good joke. He followed Dublin High School with Hamilton College where he received his bachelor's degree in economics.

Mike was accomplished in anything he pursued, due to his agile mind and creative thinking. He was in sales for many years and was a very hard worker, receiving several awards and promotions along the way. At one point, he started his own business trading currencies.

Mike loved kids and was always looking to help other people. He donated money to the 'Gesundheit Institute', believing that laughter is some of the best medicine. Mike passed away in August of 2010, after a lifetime of managing diabetes.

A plant or seed that is "dormant" is in a waiting state, suspending its life until the right conditions are available. It is not visibly active, and is seemingly asleep. One might consider death a similar experience. Perhaps Michael (1968-2010) is in such a place, waiting for the right conditions for his next adventure on earth as a human being.

Daughter Wendy left home for Skidmore College, where she double-majored in music (classical guitar) and English (poetry concentration). She went on to Emerson College in England, thinking she might become a Waldorf School teacher but decided she had had enough school and moved to St. Thomas U.S.V.I. where she worked for a potter.

In 1991, she moved to Colorado to work for Pottery by Pankratz for two years, and married in 1993. When her son and daughter were four and two she divorced, hawked her diamond wedding ring, bought a potter's wheel and a kiln, and started her business, "The Voice of Clay" (www.voiceofclay.com). She has taught many classes and lessons in numerous locations, as well as produced a full line of pottery sold across the country. She went on the get her Esthetics license in 2008 inspired by the therapeutic qualities of clay; aspiring to understand more about the body and why clay has an impact. She is now multi-certified and works part-time in a spa using Dr. Hauschka skin care, Vodder lymphatic drainage, and Reiki protocols.

In 2010, when her brother Michael passed away, she was catapulted into more spiritual endeavors. She pursued certification as a Somatic Breathwork Facilitator and Hypnosis alongside her MA in Transpersonal Psychology. Her passion lies in empowering others to be authentic through creativity and personal growth. Her children Zachary and Alexandra have both graduated from high school and are off discovering themselves and the world.

In These Woods

I was born in these woods,
Raised in these woods,
In respect and in awe
I praise in these woods.
I was young in these woods,
Had fun in these woods
Dressed up and picked berries-
Began in these woods.

Made fairy houses here
And the wolf who drew near,
Knew me and saw me as the girl
with no fear.

I followed my hood to a spot
in the woods
Where I picked loads of flowers
and herbs that taste good.
In this place sat a house with
a smoky chimney-
Had tables to rest at for coffee
and tea.

Everything handmade,
So beautifully displayed
That I wandered in awe-
I wish I had stayed.

But the sun started setting
and so was I too
So I waved goodbye smiling,
And off home I flew.

I'll never forget that Pickity Place
My Grandparents created
Guided by Grace.

-Alexandra Adinolfi

You may recognize the journey of Judith and David as the "Hero's Journey", one we have all experienced in some way. Leaving our ordinary life, we are called to adventure by choice or through crisis. Following the call, perhaps with the help of a mentor, we step into the unknown. A series of trials ensues and potentially, we face death. More often, the death is an internal process of emotional transformation. Later, when we return home from our adventure, we bring with us some element of the treasure that has transformed us to share with the world.

Our hero's story unwritten would have left David and Judith's hard work unrecognized. Pickity Place would not exist had it not been for their willingness to adventure into the unknown, their perseverance, creativity, and ability to take action.

(left) The family: Michael, David, Wendy, Andrew, Judith, Shelly circa 1988. Michael circa 1999; Michael circa 1989; Michael circa 2008. (above) Zachary Adinolfi 2016; Alexandra 2017; Alexandra as Little Red Riding Hood circa 1999.

Many would consider "Being Pickity" magical. "How did they do it?", you might ask. Well, their journey started with naivete, followed by the school of hard knocks and learning by trial and error. But, they had to start by following the heart, which requires listening. "Listening where or to what"? The answer - listening inward. Listening inward has been called many names; intuition, higher self, subconscious, transpersonal state, guidance, imagination, and gut feeling, among others. Listening to the heart is more than attending to emotions though, it is about tapping into and revering something bigger than ourselves and co-creating *with it*. For Judith and David, it was the Earth and the Spirit therein.

Listening this way means surrendering and allowing ourselves to be guided without needing to know what will happen next. It can be daunting, especially in our current culture which predominantly focuses on fear. It takes practice, trust, and faith. Starting a practice of listening can begin in many ways. While it may be trendy to say, "you can make your dreams come true", you can, if you can learn to get out of your own way.

Caroline Myss, an internationally renowned pioneer in energy medicine and an incredible teacher of archetypes, mythologies, and purpose, states in her book, *Sacred Contracts*:

"For our own good, each of us needs to learn what our mission is, because the details of how we live our lives accumulate to create health or illness. As I discovered after conducting more than eight thousand medical intuitive readings in those seventeen years, "our biography becomes our biology" – which I wrote about in Anatomy of the Spirit. *In other words, the little troubles and major traumas that we go through take up residence and live in our bodies and affect or block our energy. So it stands to reason that the further we stray from our true mission in life, the more frustrated we will become, and the more out of sync our energy will be. By coming to know your mission, you can live your life in a way that makes the best use of your energy. When you are working well with your energy, you are also making the best expression of your personal power"* [6]

David and Judith came together and distilled a vision down into reality. They didn't necessarily have the conscious thought - "I need to fulfill my life's mission", they just did what they loved. David's gift for an overarching perspective with Judith's attention to detail was the perfect combination. But - the bouquet of participants you have read about - from the family, to employees and so many others who offered their unique gifts, are what made Pickity Place. Customers brought one of the most important gifts– that of gratitude. Without all of you, Pickity Place would not continue to be thriving today.

Thank You

Writing a book - wow - it takes a village! It feels strange to claim authorship of a book so many took part in. My parents of course were integral. They sent many letters with stories and answered many, many phone calls to get the facts correct! Thanks to Linda Van de Car (my Aunt) for sharing her writing about Margaret and Carl Walter and for photos. Thanks to my siblings, Shelly and Andrew for input and information. Thanks to Bunny Paine-Clemes and Atlantic University for the writing inspiration, Sid Hall for guidance, Lance Fling for editing and Dayna Carignan for impeccable design skills! Most importantly thanks to Brian Woodbury, partner extraordinaire, who selflessly edited, encouraged, supported, took photos and advised. You amaze me. There is no way this would have come to fruition without your help!!! Thank you to the moon and back, you are my hero.

Lastly, thanks to my children, Zachary and Alexandra, who inspired me to preserve this little bit of history for future generations and who inspire me daily to be a better human being.

(left) David plowing the Pickity driveway with the tractor; Judith showcasing the Little Red Riding Hood book circa 1982.

Index

References

1. Hill, John B. (1858) *Town of Mason, NH.* Boston, MA: Lucius A. Elliot & Co.

2. Cook, Joan. (2004) *Exposed, Unbanked, Weather-beaten, Knowledge Box: The Schools of Sandwich, New Hampshire 1802- 1950.* Portsmouth, NH: Peter E. Randall

3. Baba, Meher. *Is That So?* (1978) p.113. Meher Baba Foundation

4. Salisbury, Jessie. *A Twig With Strong Roots.* (2001) Nashua Sunday Telegraph: Nashua NH.

5. Jones, Elizabeth Orton. *Little Red Riding Hood.* (1948) Golden Books; Penguin Random House: New York, NY.

6. Myss, Caroline. *Sacred Contracts.* (2002) Three Rivers Press: New York, NY